Learning and Intelligence

Learning and Intelligence

Conversations with
Skinner and Wheeler

Maureen T. Lapan
Raymond W. Houghton

IRISH ACADEMIC PRESS

Set in 11 on 13 point Ehrhardt
and published by
IRISH ACADEMIC PRESS
Kill Lane, Blackrock, Co. Dublin, Ireland
and in North America by
IRISH ACADEMIC PRESS
c/o ISBS, 5804 NE Hassalo Street, Portland, OR 97213.

A catalogue record for this title
is available from the British Library.

ISBN 0-7165-2584-4

Printed in Great Britain
by Cambridge University Press, Cambridge

To Claus Emanuel Ekstrom and Philo Theophilos Pritzkau
who taught us,
and William F. Flanagan
who employed us

Contents

Preface

The writers have lived with material in this volume for the better part of their professional careers. Its appearance in print completes a formal promise to Professors Skinner and Wheeler to share the ideas previously expressed and never diminished. Profound appreciation to both of them.

While no attempt is made to study the lives of either Professors Skinner or Wheeler, the writers have provided brief biographies of each. The former is not difficult because of his wide public image and his own autobiographical writing and the study of others. Wheeler was more difficult and the writers are particularly grateful for the assistance from Cynthia A. Shenette, Archives Librarian at Clark University, Worcester, Mass.; Andrew Martinez, Assistant Archivist at Babson College, Babson Park, Mass.; Janet Riley, Assistant Vice Chancellor for Academic Affairs at the University of Kansas, Lawrence; Professor Anthony Smith, University of Kansas, who was a colleague of Wheeler at Kansas during Wheeler's last months there; Mr Barry Eager, Berlin Memorial School, Berlin, Mass., who is town historian there; and Professor Fred Juenerman, Newkind, California.

Mr Gordon C. Rowley and Mr Peter Tobia of Rhode Island College, Providence, R.I., provided photographs of Skinner taken during a conference at the College in 1981. Mr Brendan Dempsey of Trinity College, Dublin, provided other photographs.

Ms Betsy C.L. Steinman, Campus at Lafayette, North Kingston, R.I., transcribed the interviews from the original tapes. Ms Mary Pat O'Sullivan of Trinity College, Dublin, typed the manuscript. Great service was provided by the Inter Library Loan Office, Adam Library, Rhode Island College, in acquiring difficult material in the history of psychology. Dr Lapan acknowledges the Faculty Grant Committee of Rhode Island College for their support and the College itself for research opportunity provided her during a sabbatical leave. Both writers thank Professor J.V. Rice of Trinity College, Dublin, for his continued personal support. Mr Sean Griffin, St Paul's School, Dublin, read the penultimate draft and offered many useful suggestions. Dr Paul Voorheis, Trinity College, Dublin, was most helpful with respect to modern neuroscience.

Introduction

This is a book for teachers, at least for some teachers; teachers, perhaps, like the writers themselves, who found formal courses in learning theory generally incomprehensible but were still curious as to how and why their own students learned or didn't learn. Pavlov, Watson, Thorndike, Hull, Guthrie, Koffka, Köhler, Wheeler, Skinner – all seemingly a flood of S's and R's, mazes and cages, force lines and arrows.

And then there is the question of intelligence. Is it genetically acquired or is it nurtured in environments? Each half generation raises the question anew as if it had never been asked before. Is it a serious scientific/philosophical question or is it actually a political question? In any case, it is not to say that other readers might well be interested.

At least the writers were subjected to courses in educational psychology which conceded the potential importance of studying about intelligence and learning. One wonders whether contemporary teacher training programs still offer students the same opportunity. The writers would not seriously object to persons other than teachers reading this book. Anyone interested in change in behavior might find use in these ideas.

As research students of Professor Issac Noah Thut at the University of Connecticut in 1959, the writers rather brazenly decided to confront the problem of learning and intelligence directly. Ernest Hilgard, in the introduction to his classic text, *Theories of Learning* (1948) had suggested that all learning theory fell into one of two classes: atomistic, in which learning was parts to wholes and holistic, in which learning was wholes to parts. B.F. Skinner's behaviorism was prominently featured as an atomistic theory. Among holistic theorists Hilgard had devoted an entire chapter to Raymond H. Wheeler, whom he described as the first American gestaltist. Why not phone a specialist in each category and request an interview. Simple enough. Calls were made and, naïvely, the writers were not surprised that the then 57-year-old B.F. Skinner, famous already but not as famous as he was to become, and Raymond H. Wheeler, at the time 67, somewhat famous then, yet more so than he is now, agreed to allow the writers to visit them, ask questions and tape-record an interview.

The interviews were as revelation to the writers. Much of what had been obscure and dense in print came to life for them in the personal and verbal context. Both Wheeler and Skinner had agreed to the interview if they had assurance that the material would be shared. And shared it has been. Literally thousands of students and teachers have heard the tapes since they were originally recorded. Requests for the loan of them have been received from all over the United States, as well as in Great Britain and Ireland, and continental Europe.

And so, in the Spring of 1959, the writers set off for Cambridge, Massachusetts, where they were greeted by a somewhat bemused Skinner in his cluttered office in the basement of the William James Building at Harvard University. If at any time he was flabbergasted at the audacity of the two graduate students, he never showed it. He patiently awaited the setting up of the equipment, the preparation of contents from books and note-filled briefcases, the moving of chairs in his office. He set no time limit, responding to questioning until the tape reel emptied, and then continued to discuss his views for another half hour at least, before inviting the writers to his home in Cambridge for tea, served by his wife, in his back garden beside the empty swimming pool.

During the drive from his Harvard office to his home, the conversation, begun in his office, continued and Skinner described his conviction that humankind had been under the influence of three major authority systems during what might be called "authority epochs". The first of these he called the "epoch of antiquity", in which persons looked to magical forces in nature for authority. Control was in mystical mountains, sacred lakes, animals and gnarled oak trees. He dated this period from earliest history until 4000 BC. The second epoch, which he described, was the "epoch of the Middle Ages", peculiarly dated from 4000 BC until the 17th century. Authority was in God, as represented by the Church. The third was the "epoch of Democracy" in which personkind looked to one another for authority. He dated this from the earliest days of the Enlightment until some time in the present century.

In his view, the "epoch of Democracy" had also passed. All three epochs remain, but not as dominant modalities. In that there has always been some form of control, Skinner speculated on what would be the next. Would it be pharmacological, a pill in a community's drinking water? Would it be physiological, an electrode inserted into the central nervous system? Would it be genetic manipulation or electrical/chemical balance alteration in brain cells?

He was certain that total behaviour control was imminent (5 to 1000 years?). Would it not be preferable to have personkind modified by means of the science of behaviour, whereby there might be choice through intelligence. A large part of Skinner's later writing and lecturing dealt with these critical issues. It was in the science of human behaviour that Skinner saw a path to the solution of the problems of humankind and the global environment.

Skinner had the opportunity to hear his own interview twenty years later. While visiting Rhode Island College in Providence, Rhode Island in 1981 where he spoke at a colloquium on the topic, "Is There a Philosophy of Behaviorism?", he recalled the 1959 interview and requested the interviewers to play it for him. He sat in the lounge of the philosophy department attentively listening to the original interview with dozens of academic spectators watching. When the tape ended, he looked up and said to the writers, "I haven't changed very much, have I?" They were relieved to be able to say, "No, Fred, you haven't."

Two weeks after the original Skinner interview, the writers travelled to Babson Institute of Business Administration, now Babson College, in Wellesley Hills, Massachusetts to visit R.H. Wheeler. The interview took place in the living room of Wheeler's home preceded by a visit to his office and a personally conducted tour of the Babson campus.

The writers were surprised at the time to learn that Wheeler had been, and continued to be, engaged in an extended period of research developing data and theory relating to world weather cycles and human behaviour. He indicated that a portion of his income was derived from the utilization of data from the study of weather cycles for prediction of business trends and that he had worked at Babson primarily to sit in on meetings of a think-tank which prepared forecasts of business trends for a Babson monthly newsletter servicing business subscribers.

Wheeler, therefore, was somewhat surprised and pleased that the writers were there to query him about his original work as the founder of organismic psychology. As he warmed to the interview he became genuinely excited. He laughed often and seemed interested to reconstruct ideas which had interested him twenty five years earlier. There was little question of his continued commitment to his earlier thinking.

The writers had been interested to note that, while Hilgard had devoted a whole chapter to Wheeler in his 1948 edition of *Theories of Learning*, he had been all but exorcised from the 1956 edition, the discussion of his work having been reduced to a footnote in chapter 7, "Classical Gestalt Theory". They wondered why.

In spite of the simple fact that Wheeler seemed to have moved from his earlier interests and, unlike Skinner, had not undertaken experimental verification of his work, they continued to wonder why.

Hilgard (1964) suggests that "research on or related to the position (Wheeler's) was no longer sufficient to call for a new chapter." He asked

> Does this mean that the ideas which seemed so fresh when Wheeler and Perkins presented them in 1932 are valueless in 1964? Not at all; it means that something was wrong with the manner in which the ideas were developed, so that strong contemporary defenders are not to be found.
>
> Hilgard (1964), pp. 65–66

Further detail regarding Wheeler's removal from the various editions of Hilgard's text can be found in the appendix. The writers have always felt that Wheeler's experimental work with "hot and cold rats" described in the 1959 interview, had proved an embarrassment to his colleagues as he flew in the face of scholarly "correctness" in his defence of Lamarck's principles of heredity. It was reported in a then-contemporary release from the morgue files of the University of Kansas that, "Dr Wheeler's findings … have not made him particularly popular with members of the history staff at the university". Mendelian/Darwinian thinking on heredity and evolution had come to dominate academic thinking even though there had been an enthusiastic defence of Lamarck's position on heritable characteristics. Cannon (1959)

Wheeler claimed that self-initiated physical changes in organisms would be passed on to ensuing generations. In the light of contemporary scholarly belief, this might have proved embarrassing. Stephen Jay Gould, in a June 1994 conversation with the writers, dismissed any possibility of usefulness in Wheeler's faith in Lamarck. "He was just wrong", Gould stated.

Wheeler's later weather cycle research might have also alienated his academic fellows. In what has seemed to the writers as an attempt at theory on a grand scale, Wheeler, in an ambitious effort to relate historical epochs with weather cycles, was probably the object of derision by other academics. It is suggested that the Babson business trends newsletter had enough faith in Wheeler to bring him to the institute and support his research activity. One is reminded of the devotion shown to Buckminster Fuller by international influentials. It was almost as if they were saying to themselves, "This person may be a little idiocyncratic, but suppose he's right?"

A third factor in the loss of interest in Wheeler may have been in the personality and temperament of the man himself. Hartman (1974) notes that psychologists representing alternative positions found gestaltists, among whom he included Wheeler, personally difficult to deal with as well as flouters of conventional practice. Wheeler was quick, fanciful and spontaneous in his thinking. He probably became bored with an idea as soon as he expressed it, however bright and promising the ideas might have been. Unlike Skinner who was always the detail person, even finding it necessary to pursue an idea to conclusion literally inventing the necessary technology. Wheeler, as in his theory of learning, was interested only until he had obtained insight. For him, insight was sufficient. Verification was incidental. Is there any wonder that academics found Raymond Wheeler too whimsical for their taste?

Given the writers' primary interest in the study of learning theory and educational psychology, both interviews were structured so as to generate responses which would deal with issues related to questions faced by teachers and students. Therefore, the topics introduced into the interviews focused on these items: the nature of man/person, intelligence and individual differences, the learning process, memory and forgetting, and evaluation of learning.

The juncture at which the interviewers introduced the questions dealing with the topics varied from interview to interview. In each interview, however, all of the topics were addressed so that the reader would have straightforward access to the contrasting points of view of the psychologists.

The character of the interviews reflects the theoretical base upon which each of the interviewees constructed his psychology. The interviews are recorded here in their entirety, including diversions from the central interview themes as they more fully represent the views of Skinner and Wheeler.

In addition to the interviews themselves, the writers have added commentary based on their own study and experience, in effect, a second conversation. Further, a review of Skinner's and Wheeler's writings was undertaken so that specific reference could be provided to the publications which treat the points raised in the interviews. These references are supplied so that the reader may readily locate readings which would extend the material included in the interviews. They constitute a rather detailed annotated bibliography of the relevant sources. While the Skinner material should be easily obtainable in any good library, the Wheeler sources may be somewhat difficult to locate.

Skinner's first text, *The Behavior of Organisms; An Experimental Analysis*, was published in 1938. Since its publication, Skinner has produced eighteen books. Three of these eighteen are autobiographical, and one a commentary on old age, as well as *Notebooks*, a volume of selected noted edited by Robert Epstein. In addition, he has produced a steady stream of journal articles and lectures.

Wheeler's first book, *The Science of Psychology*, was published in 1929. This publication was followed by four books as well as many journal articles on an extraordinarily wide range of topics. R.H. Wheeler died in 1961; hence, the interview included here is probably the last interview in which his considerations on learning were addressed.

An extended bibliography of all of the texts mentioned in the book is also included. For every idea and controversy mentioned readers are provided with at least an entry source of follow up material.

The writers hope that the readers will find invitation to join in the conversation as they have themselves. Multiple readings of the interviews have seemed to accentuate the differences in the two psychological positions. Surprisingly, extended readings also seem to suggest that Skinner and Wheeler are describing similar phenomena using different metaphors.

And remember, that while the writers have done all that they were capable of doing to assure the accuracy of the reporting and the respectability of the reactions, they remain school teachers, not scientists nor historians. As such, they assume responsibility for all that might be found here.

I. Biographical Sketches

Biographical sketches of B.F. Skinner and R.H. Wheeler are included here to provide some general information about the psychologists, the schools of thought they represent, and some contextual elements for the interviews and the responses to them.

Skinner published his own three-volume autobiography; hence, many details of his life are readily accessible. The writers have made use of Skinner's personal abridged biography appearing in Epstein (1982), originally written for E.G. Boring and G. Lindsey (1967, pp. 387–413). Wheeler, less well known than Skinner, left no autobiographical notes, details of his formation as a psychologist, or of his later years. The data reported here were obtained through librarians and archivists at the college and universities where Wheeler studied and was employed as well as through personal interviews with former colleagues.

It is intended that these sketches will introduce the reader to the scientists, their thoughts, and their place in the course of development of western psychological and social development.

SKINNER

B.F. Skinner's own life was a prime example of an individual in response to the contingencies of reinforcement which shaped him. "Why?" would be to ask the non-behavioral question. No one controller directed his shaping. No controller conceptualised the operant movement of his growth. Yet, his life did seem a product of the major contingent possibilities. On a world scale, Skinner's life was played out within a range of perhaps ever narrowing possibilities.

To believe his own autobiographical perception, Skinner grew up in a Norman Rockwell world of snapshot, not video, images of life in early 20th-century America. What does he remember selectively? He is not impressed with his forebears, especially on his father's side. He did seem "proud" of his ancestor, Captain Potter, who had fought under Washington, contrary to his stated belief that "pride" has no justification. He also seemed embarrassed by his father's hunger for praise. In describing his father's sense of failure as "secret" suffering from his mother's ambitions, was he not making an unconscious rather than behavioral analysis of his father's condition?

He seemed quite happy with his Tom Sawyer childhood in Susquehanna, Pennsylvania. He built things. He explored places. He "liked" school. He had good "no nonsense" mathematics texts (non-programmed?). He had bad science, but did "experiments" at home. He was surrounded by books "beautifully bound", if commercial.   He had an inspirational teacher in Mary Graves who taught him in many fields including Old Testament and literature.

He was an amateur musician who did not know the difference between a cornet and a trumpet and naively thought that ensemble playing of popular music was jazz. His grandmother showed him a conception of hell in the parlor stove. Miss Graves introduced him to a metaphoric reading of the Bible. He shared with Miss Graves what was to be a terminal loss of faith. He found childhood seemingly happy but mildly aversive, mouth washed out with soap (once), warnings from the father about "criminal minds" resulting in his being "afraid of the police". His mother seemed to have said, "Tut, Tut" a lot. His school report card indicated that he "annoyed others". He also remembered being a problem to the school janitor he wanting to be "let in early". Could it have been to avoid the "congregation of students" outside?

During his sophomore year at Hamilton College, he discovered and described what he felt family life should really be like. There he met the Saunders family who modelled a pre-*Walden Two* utopia, with evening soirees of high culture, intellectual and artistic house guests, letters from Ezra Pound, all providing positive reinforcement contingencies for the immature Skinner.

He never "fitted in" to student life at Hamilton, but the experience again provided contingencies enabling the emerging Skinner to be shaped in contrast to his perception of the mundane inferior environment of the college. He tormented the college establishment with a series of patronising tricks and practical jokes which confirmed his superior view of himself. Ironically, he recalled that all of his courses had been of some use to him.

Behavior learned through his relationship with his schoolteacher, Miss Graves, had not been extinguished by the time he had graduated from Hamilton. He devoted the next two years of his life to beginning a writing career. The period was so unproductive that he remarked that the Federal Bureau of Investigation had been curious about the "two year gap" in his life. He went to Greenwich Village for "six months of Bohemian living", and a summer in Paris before graduate school at Harvard. He had failed as a writer for lack of "something to say". He felt also that "a writer might portray human behavior accurately, but he (the writer) did not therefore understand it". If he, himself, were to remain interested in the human condition he would "turn to the scientific". "The relevant science appeared to be psychology though I had only the vaguest idea of what it meant!"

He had studied no psychology as an undergraduate although, through his biology teacher at Hamilton, he had been exposed to Loeb's *Psychology of the Brain* and *Comparative Psychology*, and Pavlov's *Conditioned Reflexes*. On his own he had read Bertrand Russell's *Outline of Philosophy* in which he described Watson's *Behaviorism*, especially the epistemological implications. His literary readings raised in him broad questions of human behavior and it was "only extraordinary luck which kept me from becoming a gestalt or (so help me) a COGNITIVE PSYCHOLOGIST!!" (his emphasis).

No worry on either account. Graduate school at Harvard did not seem to result in enthusiastic study of academic psychology although he did systematically read psychology and physiology. His professor, E.G. Boring, was on leave. He seemed to have been influenced by the weekly colloquiums and particularly by his relationships with S.J. Crozier and Hudson Hoagland in the Department of General Psychology. He received his Ph.D. without the support of Boring. He actually manifested his continuing contempt for institutional authority by bating Boring, challenging him to reject his thesis. Boring took up no challenge, but stepped off Skinner's committee. He took the Ph.D. in 1931, having spent much of his time in the physiology laboratory.

After five years as a junior fellow at Harvard, Skinner moved to the University of Minnesota where "for the first time I began to learn college psychology" in order to stay "... a jump or two ahead of my students!!!" He was extremely proud of his teaching at Minnesota. He began work on *Verbal Behavior*, did wartime experimentation on the use of pigeons to guide missiles, invented his aircrib as an environment for rearing infants and began the writing of *Walden Two*. In the autumn of 1945 he moved to the chair of the Department of Psychology at Indiana. In 1948 he returned permanently to Harvard.

Skinner's publication of *The Behavior of Organisms* (1948) placed him at the forefront of Western psychology and became the foundation for his lifelong work as the twentieth century's spokesman for radical behaviorism. His thinking became the focus of interest of an audience beyond that of professional psychology through the publication of his novel, *Walden Two* (1948), which extended the principles of behaviorism to the design of society. Beginning as a cult book on college campuses, it gradually attracted a wider readership. A million copies of *Walden Two* were sold and, in 1970, a new hard cover edition was published by the Literary Guild followed by another edition in 1976, with a new preface by Skinner.

In 1971, *Beyond Freedom and Dignity* appeared. His scientific approach to the study of human behavior and his application of behavioral principles to the shaping of individuals and society engendered strong controversy in both the popular press as well as the professional literature. *Beyond Freedom and Dignity* was on the *New York Times* best-seller list for twenty weeks. Skinner was called upon to respond to professional and public criticism and questions on radio and television thereby providing him a forum for the discussion of behaviorism, psychology and education. Unlike R.H. Wheeler, Skinner's name and his ideas had high recognition during the 60s, 70s and 80s.

There was no question that Skinner viewed himself as subject. He described "manipulating his own behavior" (a different phenomenon than "will"?) by creating the contingency conditions which would be reinforcing to his self-determined appropriate behavior. He would claim that his willingness to publish three volumes of autobiography intimately, if selectively, divulging facts of his life, was evidence of his desire to study and make available to others, his perception of his own behavior as a scientist. One cannot but be bemused by his alleged fear of "ghosts" which he wished to purge from consideration in explanation of phenomena. Is his own need for personal control betrayed in his claims of self-determination of his own behavior as person and as scientist?

It is no denial of his radical behavioral position to suggest that there was no more "freedom and dignity" in Fred Skinner than there was, as he claimed, in any organism. He was born with a genetic history. He was born into an environment in which the contingencies were naturally reinforcing. He claimed that he arranged contingencies in such a way as to be reinforcing to the behaviors which he determined worthy. As a child and, to a great extent as an adult, he behaved at Kohlberg's first stage of conventional behavior. Kohlberg (1981), pp. 409–412. At the surface level, Skinner, from childhood by his own description, behaved as a "nice boy", totally within the expectation of a child born into 19th-century American conventionalism.

He spoke of arranging (his) environment "in which what would otherwise be hard work is actually effortless". Would that the contingencies were such that everyone could.

All of his work was done "playfully".

> ... almost all noted scientists follow a "hedonistic ethic." I have been powerfully reinforced by many things: food, sex, music, art, and literature – and my scientific results. I have built apparatuses as I have painted pictures or modelled figures in clay. I have conducted experiments as I have played the piano. I have written scientific papers and books as I have written stories and poems. I have never designed and conducted an experiment because I felt I ought to do so, or to meet a deadline, or to pass a course, or to "publish rather than perish". I dislike experimental designs which will not be reinforcing until they have been exhaustively analyzed.
>
> I freely change my plans when richer reinforcements beckon. My thesis was written before I knew it was a thesis. *Walden Two* was not planned at all. I may practice self-management for Protestant reasons, but I do so in such a way as to maximize non-Protestant reinforcements. I emphasize positive contingencies.
>
> Epstein (1982), p. 30

Skinner's later life grand plan was to explain everything. Was his wish for society and individuals to influence the direction of behavioral change through intelligence an attempt to combat the heretofore inevitability of behavior shaping through accidental (or perhaps incidental) contingencies? The will he denies becomes the vehicle for the creation of his Walden, for is not planning the product of that selfsame will? Other grand theorists have fallen victim to the belief that they themselves might avoid the inevitability of the very theoretical condition which they had posited.

Whether or not Skinner was able "to play" at his own behavior through control of personal contingency environments and whether or not he deserved dignity if he were merely living out a life of response through a set of unplanned and/or uncontrolled operants, Skinner managed to achieve, impress, and influence his century. For, like Freud and a few others, when human behavior is to be explained in ordinary life, in fiction, in history, whatever; some suggest the unconscious, some suggest God's will and a whole lot of others say Skinner's behaviorism.

WHEELER BIOGRAPHY

Raymond Holder Wheeler isn't known much any more. In some ways he is the old soldier, stripped of his medals. And yet he is listed in Zusne's (1975), *Names in the History of Psychology*, rated 19 out of 27 possible points, meaning a peer jury recognised his name, knew his contribution and some considered him among the top 500 psychologists, 1600–1975.

Wheeler was important in the early 1930s. His text on educational psychology, *Principles of Mental Development* (1932) with F. Theodore Perkins, his twenty-three year old student and disciple, provided progressive education with an appropriate psychology. Watson's behaviorism and Thorndike's connectionism had not suited. They were too mechanistic, too undemocratic, too static, too pessimistic to match the then vital, dynamic, hopeful, democratic philosophy of progressivism.

Gestalt psychology, to which Wheeler turned, had its impetus in Germany with the big three of Max Wertheimer, Wolfgang Köhler and Kurt Koffka. The gestaltists brimmed with confidence. It was as if they had invented a new science, beyond psychology. The possibilities of gestalt thinking for educational psychology were recognised. By 1924 Koffka had been translated into English by Robert Morris Ogden of Cornell University. He had written a chapter on gestalt in his own text, *Psychology and Education* (1926). He saw gestalt as a possible resolution of the controversy among connectionism, behaviorism and psychological pragmatism which had precluded any fulfilment of James admonition to teachers that "... teaching must everywhere agree with psychology". James (1899), pp. 21–27

Gestalt, simply meaning whole, had been simmering for a decade. Koffka, Wertheimer and Köhler had introduced it in their visits to America. All three assumed distinguished positions in prominent U.S. universities. While Boyd Bode (1929), the great spokesman for Progressivism, had anticipated the potential, it remained for Wheeler, then at the University of Kansas, to articulate an original organismic position in his four books published between 1929 and 1932. They served as the rationalised psychology of the progressive movement.

Raymond Holder Wheeler was a New Englander, born in Berlin, Massachusetts, 9 March 1892, on a 70-acre dairy farm established by his grandfather. His father, Henry Arthur, was a self-confident, opinionated though apparently agreeable farmer of some standing, active in the local Congregational church. His mother, Nellie Reed Wheeler, was a Quaker. He grew up on the family farm in what was then rural New England. He must have had organ lessons in the Congregational church attended by his father as music and organ performance continued as major interest for him throughout his life. He retained ties to Berlin and was known to contemporary citizens in the town as the professor who liked to "walk the walls" of the old farm up until the time of the death of his parents and even beyond, as his sister, Amelia Dunfield, continued to live in the homestead.

Worcester, a prosperous city in central Massachusetts, was the site of Clark College cum graduate university. G. Stanley Hall and John W. Baird were teaching psychology there. Hall, who had taught Dewey at Johns Hopkins University, brought Sigmund Freud to America to lecture at Clark in 1909. Earlier, in 1900, Charles Sanders Pierce, who had been a colleague of Hall during his brief lectureship at Johns Hopkins, applied for, and was refused, a lectureship at Clark by Hall who was then President of the university.

Wheeler matriculated at Clark in 1909, the very year of Freud's visit although psychoanalysis never seems to have particularly influenced him. There is limited discussion of it in his writing. He studied general psychology, theory of evaluation and genesis of the mind in his second year, together with genetic psychology, sociology, physics and a second course in evaluation during his final year. He took the AB degree in 1912.

The *Clark College Monthly* (1912) described Wheeler as involved in

> ... his eager climb to the top of the psychological ladder. Ray has struggled through college, carrying all possible work, music and college activities. Yet he loves a good "rough house" and his laugh is proverbial. After adding certain parts of the alphabet to his name, he intends to teach.

> (p. 532)

Wheeler was enrolled as a graduate student in the Department of Psychology from September 1912 to June 1915. He was awarded the Master of Arts Degree in 1913 and the degree Doctor of Philosophy in 1915. He took courses with Hall in Psychology of Feelings and Emotions, Psychogenesis and Psychoanalysis. He studied the Process of Learning, Imagination and Memory with John W. Baird and Educational Psychology with William H. Burnham.

Hall was, of course, a leading psychologist of his time, famous for his work in child study, developmental psychology, and perhaps infamous for his devotion to genetic determinism, the particulars of which would be considered racist today. There was no direct evidence to believe the student followed his professor. In fact Wheeler was to write much later,

> ... it is easy for surrounding nations to kill the soul of a race by making intolerable its intercourse with environment as for society to kill the soul of an individual. There is social as well as an individual dementia praecox. Imperialism and religious proselytising have demonstrated this repeatedly. When a superior or powerful race forces education and religion upon an inferior or weaker race the same situation results. Thus we see the importance of mutual tolerance and non-interference in international affairs.
>
> Wheeler (1931), pp. 221–222

Wheeler spent the late spring and early autumn of 1913 visiting universities in Scotland, England, France, Germany, Belgium, Holland and Switzerland. According to a University of Kansas biographical sheet written by Helen Tatum (1927), Wheeler visited

> productive psychological laboratories, studying their equipment and getting a line on the research work and method of conducting classes.

Did Wheeler visit Wertheimer, Köhler, Koffka or Lewin at this time? The writers do not know. Wheeler's later work at Oregon was to be involved with perception in the blind. Did he discuss psychoanalysis while in Europe? Hall most certainly could have opened doors for him.

He returned to Clark late in 1913 shortly before the start of war in Europe. He served as a laboratory assistant and as a special research fellow during his last year at Clark. Through the good auspices of Dr J.P. Porter of Clark, Wheeler obtained his first teaching position at the University of Oregon in the autumn of 1915. In an unpublished letter to Professor C.S. Conklin, University of Oregon, Eugene, Oregon, 15 April 1915, Porter described Wheeler as

> ... the best to be found in ability, training and interest. While his interests ... are rather narrow, being confined to experimental psychology alone. While somewhat immature in manner and judgement I believe that Dr Wheeler will proceed in adapting himself, at least after a little time, in the requirements of the position.

Wheeler had married Ruth Dunlop of Worcester in 1915. They were to have one child, Lois Dunlap Wheeler. In a personal biographical sketch, he reported his only surviving relative to be Mrs Amelia Dunfield of Berlin, Massachusetts, a Congregationalist (biographical sketch for the University of Kansas Files, *c.*1932). He accepted the appointment to the University of Oregon in 1915 and was to remain there until 1925 except for the period of the U.S. involvement in World War I.

In an unpublished letter dated 20 August 1916, from Oregon, he told of his hiking in "Snake River Canyon and the Moscow Mountains", of seeing the "Three Sisters (mountains) at the head of the McKenzie Valley". He described his facilities ...

> My own (office), a lecture room and a seminar room, and one room fitted up as a shop but ... suitable for experimental purposes, and ... an excellent dark room. We have direct and indirect current in each room and also compressed air and gas. Owing to a lack of funds in the past we have not very much good apparatus as yet. I have four divisions in elementary psychology and two laboratories. I tried an experiment last semester – gave a course in the psychology of music. This year I am going to give an advanced course in systematic psychology.

He put his musical background to advantage involving himself in productions of the *Seven Last Words of Christ* at the Philharmonic Society. With no orchestra available they "... asked me to take the score and work out the parts played on the various instruments and use appropriate organ stops, thus making the organ do the work of an orchestra. After the performance (with himself at the organ) people remarked that it was the best thing given in Eugene for years."

At Oregon he undertook research on perception in blind persons. He reported in a letter to Porter, 25 October 1916,

> ... it seems that such illusions as the Müller-Lyer, lengths of horizontal and vertical lines, squares, triangles, and the like, are as easily obtained by means of touch and hand movements in the case of the blind, as they are obtained thru the vision in sighted people; moreover, the illusions seem to be provoked for the same reasons as in sighted people. He is also studying the effect of placing the objects at different angles, the effect of passive and active movements on the strength of the illusions, the effect of visualizing the objects, and the

like. Another problem involves the question of the importance of kinaesthetic imagery in learning new motor coordinations, the effect of visual images and various instructions on learning. A third is devoted to ways and means of presenting memorial material to the blind for the most rapid and accurate learning; a fourth is calculated to throw light on a series of mental tests for blind children.

In the same letter he mentioned an "offer from Titchener this summer." (Titchener of Cornell, who would later be criticised by Wheeler as being mechanistic.) He told of delivering a paper on the Freudian view of dreams and gave seminars on "higher intellectual process, Skeffington's experiments for reflexes and the like."

He served in the Army from September 1917 to January 1919. By his own testimony letter, 5 May 1918, from Camp Bowie, Fort Worth, Texas, to Dr J.P. Porter, he became a Captain in the Sanitary Corps., was on a committee for construction of intelligence tests at the Surgeon General's Office, presumably the Army Alpha Examination, served in the School of Military Psychology in Georgia and was the chief of psychological service at Camp Bowie, Texas. He reported to Porter in the letter that:

> I am in charge of the examining here, and so far my time has been spent in getting a building, in fitting up an office and getting my supplies together to begin examining shortly.

After returning from military service during the period 1920–1925, while still at Eugene, Wheeler published continuously on synaesthesia, theories of will, visual phenomena with the blind, meaning, the static and the dynamic in logic of science. Beginning in 1925 his publications turned to problems of intelligence. He wrote on freedom vs. determinism in the distinguished publication, *Monist*. The same year saw a series of articles in the *Psychological Review* on systematic psychology. In 1925 he left Oregon and moved to the University of Kansas where he was to remain until 1947.

Wheeler's bibliography lists no published works in the two years after his arrival in Kansas. He came as professor "in charge of the psychological section of the department of Philosophy and the Logic of Science" (Tatum, 1927). His publications void, 1926–1927, after a continuous flow of articles and reports in his post-World War I years at Oregon, was doubtless part due to settling into a new position in a new and very different location half-way across the United States. The plains of Kansas are a very different environment from the familiar green rolling hills of central Massachusetts and the dramatic natural setting of Eugene, Oregon. It was the calm before the storm. In the four years 1929–1932 he would publish four major works, now nearly ignored, but in their time not only a prodigious output, but received as providing a psychological rationalization for an era. In 1929 there appeared *The Science of Psychology, Readings in Psychology* (1930), *The Laws of Human Nature* (1931), and in 1932 the psychological Bible of progressivism, *Principles of Mental Development.*

The move to a new setting had certainly been one factor in the pause in his earlier output. A second and perhaps more important reason, was that Wheeler seems to have shifted his own intellectual gears. Understanding this shift must await a more dedicated investigation of Wheeler's personal and intellectual development. There is no doubt that the decade of the 1920's provided a cauldron of ideas to stimulate his thinking. The impact of new thought from various areas of science were being felt and recognised. The world had lived with 65 years of reaction to Darwin. Gould (1991), pp. 312–318, described the early reactionary attitudes in American academia led by the legendary Louis Agassiz at Harvard. Recovery of Mendel's genetic research was 25 years old. Physics had been undergoing fantastic growth with the emergence of quantum mechanics which would provide new metaphors and symbols for the new century. Einstein, himself the great revolutionary, was resisting a final break with Newtonian positivism with his general and special theories of relativity.

Psychology, scientific psychology, had been in the process of escaping the comfortable womb of philosophy. Sociology and social psychology were a step further behind in scientific identity. In America, psychology was in crisis of identity and direction. There was the behaviorism of John Watson. His *Behaviorism* (1915, revised 1930) was in conflict with the Connectionism of Edward Lee Thorndike for acceptance as the true psychology. Somehow, the psychoanalytic theories, introduced to America at the great gathering at Clark in 1909 when Hall brought Freud to America, had not found comfortable acceptance within the scientific psychological community.

Wheeler had been writing extensively on synaesthesia and meaning. His interest in perception was well established. In his travels in Europe a decade earlier he may well have encountered the most recent and positive considerations of gestalt. Wertheimer had published his work on the phi-phenomenon in 1912.

Gestalt thinking, of course, was not new. Hartman (1935/1974, pp. 10–80) discusses the origins. Ehrenfel's *On Wholeness in Music* (Dithey,

1894), with the idea that neither introspection nor experiment could reveal the nature of mind, only "examination of a man's history"; William James (1890) expressed the view that "No one ever had a simple sensation by itself"; Dewey's (1896) rejection of the reflex arc; Helmholtz' work early in the century on physiological optics; Rubin's work on experimental phenomenology; Wertheimer, Koffka and Köhler, together with Kurt Lewin all had been together in Germany. Koffka's *Growth of the Mind* was translated to English in 1924, but it seems apparent in his development that Wheeler had known the work earlier.

Each of the three spoke fluent English and travelled and lectured in America. Koffka settled in Smith College, Köhler at Swarthmore and Wertheimer at the New School for Social Research. Did Wheeler know them, hear them, read them? Again the details of his intellectual development remain for further researchers, but he knew their work and seems to have been particularly influenced by Koffka. Ogden had translated Koffka's *Growth of the Mind* in 1924 and had included an important chapter on Gestalt in his text *Psychology and Education* (1926). Boyd Bode (1929), *Conflicting Psychologies of Learning* saw gestalt as a solution to the inadequacies of connectionism and behaviorism. And, of course, there had been Dewey, who described a psychology, a philosophy, and a total spirit which fitted his era. Thorndike, whom Hilgard described as having "... his scientific foot in the twentieth century and his moral foot in the nineteenth", simply had not matched the times. Social Darwinism, alive and well since the 1870s when the idea had been popularised by Herbert Spencer posited a fixed and determined mind which did not suit. Psychologies which offered hope through the possibilities of learning were more agreeable to the age.

Another major influence in the development of organismic theory was to be found in biology and evolutionary theory. Coghill's (1928) *Anatomy and the Problem of Behavior* in which he established the idea of individuation and differentiation having root in mass action was particularly powerful. C.M. Child's idea of the transmission of energy in organisms interested him. Herbert Spencer Jennings' Lamarckian conception of evolution in which hereditary characteristics become changed by environmental conditions, coloured Wheeler's thinking. He was abreast of contemporary physics. He welcomed the uncertainty principle. He found analogies in quantum mechanics. He resolved to purge all dualisms, which he saw as the scourge of understanding. Structure and function, he felt, were simply two expressions of the same thing. Like Berkeley before him, he eliminated the need for discrete matter. Everything, in his mind, reverted to the laws of human nature, eight of which he described and extended in *The Laws of Human Nature* (1931) his most important book. In a basic statement of the laws he claimed that they offered an explanation for everything both physical and mental. "The laws of dynamics describe, in universal terms, the behavior of energy systems."

He begins his laws of human nature without identifying their source although they may have had inspiration in Köhler. Both Thorndike and Watson had offered the possibilities of learning, but were too mechanistic. The ideas of gestalt, proclaimed with an evangelical zeal, seemed more promising. Wheeler's Laws are listed in appendix C.

Wheeler then extended the basic *Laws of Human Nature* to his Laws of Perception, to Laws of Learning and Laws of Personality, in effect, developing, for him, a total system. He would further extend this total psychological system to an educational psychology to service the Progressive Education conceived by Dewey and surely imperfectly incorporated into the schools of America, Cremin (1961). *The Principles of Mental Development* (1932) capped a productive stretch of output that may match, with the sole exception of Dewey himself, any in the history of education in this century. Hartman's (1935/1974) treatment of Wheeler's material would be of great usefulness to teachers.

By 1932 he had said all that he had to say about psychology and education, although he would revise his *Science of Psychology* in 1940. Already, by 1938, he had plunged into a new passion, the belief that, through a titanic analysis, he could find the external force of weather cycles decisively effecting human behavior so decisively as to determine the course of history. Further, through the determination of these cycles, one might project the future course of world events.

It is not the task of this volume to follow Wheeler's strange and exaggerated vision through the next thirty years. To satisfy the reader's curiosity it is enough to say that Wheeler related what he perceived to be cycles of world events, to the newly decipherable cycles of world weather. Using 96 research assistants, provided through the National Youth Administration, he began to develop his *Big Book* in which he incorporated a vast store of data relating to his cycles. The gigantic book, seven and a half feet across, weighed over 200 pounds, and contains a huge amount of data hand-written in color coded columns. His publications on the material began in 1938 and continued to his death.

Wheeler left the University of Kansas in the early part of 1947 under not usual circumstances. He spent one year at Erskine College in South Carolina before returning to New England and a position as professor of psychology at Babson Institute in Massachusetts, presumably to continue his research and to work on a projection of business cycles for Babson.

When the writers encountered him there in 1959 he was still deeply involved in his cycles research. On first meeting him, being shown around the college and viewing his hundreds of boxes of research files, they thought they had the wrong man. As he described his research in the rapid fire enthusiasm of a true believer, the writers looked at each other and shrugged. "And are you still interested in learning theory?" they asked. "Oh, that's why you're here", he said and immediately shifted his enthusiasm to discussing work about which he had been excited 25 years earlier. He thought back to 1930, and as in his own theory of memory, began to reproduce the experience with a modest deterioration of perceptual detail, but with no diminuition of energy under the tension "... of constructing a stimulus-pattern partly duplicating the original (condition)". In an instant he was back in Kansas in 1930 replicating his early ideas for the writers. There was no loss of passion for Wheeler was a man of passion. He had described emotion as,

> ... not (a) special discrete kind of behavior ... It is an aspect of whatever the person is doing at the time, when, in the approach to a given goal, the tension is increased and maintained through intraorganic stimulation. ... Emotive behavior is any intentional, intelligent behavior, energised.
>
> Wheeler (1932), p. 207

He wrote with the selfsame passion at the conclusion of *The Laws of Human Nature* (1931),

> Danger lies in the ranks of the scientists who cry:– "Experiment, don't think", for this is the cry of intellectual suicide. Danger lies in the ranks of the clergy who say:– "Believe, don't think", and in the ranks of teachers whose methods imply, "This is authority, the truth will not stand alone." Danger lies in the casting all but statistical meaning in science to the wind.
>
> (p. 224)

> The scientist must know his philosophy. The philosopher must know his science; the clergyman and the teacher must know both.
>
> (p. 227)

Raymond Wheeler died 24 August 1961.

II. Interviews, Commentary and References

Readers will find that in most cases footnotes provide commentary to material in the interviews. Bullet points (•) refer to items for further reference.

B.F. Skinner delivering his keynote address at a colloquim Is There a Philosophy of Behaviorism? *at Rhode Island, 1981. R.I.C. photo by Peter Tobia.*

R.W.H.   We are fortunate enough to be at Harvard University today and in the office of Prof. B.F. Skinner. Prof. Skinner has been good enough to give us his time to discuss some aspects of his work and thought.

Dr Skinner, could we first of all ask you, basically and according to your approaches, what do you assume to be the nature of man? Could we put it this way? Is it possible that you might adopt a scientific viewpoint of being able to observe only behavior, and at the same time have reservations in which you might believe some things that you cannot assume in beginning scientific study?

B.F.S.   That is beginning a long ways back, on philosophical issues. I am approaching the funnel of education from a lot of other research and behavior, most of which was done on the lower, so-called lower animals, and you can't really study them in a scientific way unless you assume that there is nothing capricious about their behavior.[1]

Suddenly an animal can take it into his head and go and do something else and then you can't very well get scientifically regular results. You cannot get lawful observations. Now, it has been our experience that as we learn more about an organism and tighten up our experimental control, that which looks like capriciousness disappears[2] and that the behavior is orderly and at times very remarkably so, and even when quite complex.

---

1   Skinner simply declares that organisms tend to behave non-capriciously. This is discerned in the careful observation of behavior. He posits no explanation as to why behavior tends to be non-capricious. Wheeler, contrastingly, would explain "non capricious behavior" as being the result of his so-called organismic laws. He begins *before* the behavior with the "laws" which generate the behavior which can be none other than non-capricious. Skinner begins *after* the behavior with no attempt at prior account.

2   The idea of non-capricious behavior was discussed further in conversation with Skinner at his home. He cited the example of large numbers of spectators attending sporting events or popular musical concerts. With careful planning, perhaps as few as a dozen specialist security personnel can control,

33

Now, man may be different, but again it is a good working assumption to assume that we are only dealing with part of biology in some very broad sense.[3] Everything that man does is done by him as a organism with, of course, a genetic history and that the people will differ very much as their genetic history differs, and with a personal history. He has had an absolutely unique experience from birth and each of us is, I am sure, entirely unique. That does not mean that we have spontaneous capacities to change courses mid-stream here.[4] We have to behave in a way which is deter-

---

within limits, the behavior of many thousands of spectators without the necessity of rigid fencing or the display of aversive implements (bull horns, batons, weaponry). Intelligent planning, together with subtle interventional strategies, are able to effect remarkably predictable specific mass behavior. Under normal circumstances even large numbers of individuals behave non-capriciously.

Julian Jaynes (1976), *The Origin of Consciousness and The Breakdown of the Bicameral Mind*, in his analysis of the "non conscious" functioning of organisms in ordinary life, reminds us that, most of the time, organisms function purely behaviorally and non-idiosyncratically, driven by genetic (biological) predisposition or learned (historical) precedent.

Interestingly, Wheeler, in the following interview (p. 70, note 2) likewise assumes non-capriciousness in his discussion of so-called organismic "laws".

- B.F. Skinner (1968), *Technology of Teaching*, p. 84 and pp. 225–226, presents a discussion of objections to the study of animal behavior as a step in the analysis of human behavior. Chapter 1, "The Etymology of Teaching", pp. 1–8, discusses three metaphors traditionally used to account for human behavior as well as three theories of learning. The concept of the "storage machines" of the mind is treated within the context of the chapter, see pp. 2–3; p. 204 provides an additional brief commentary on the same subject.

- — (1971) *Beyond Freedom and Dignity*, Chapter 9, "What is Man?" p. 211, defines man within a scientific context. Chapter 9, "What is Man?", pp. 201–222 discusses the use of lower organisms for the study of behavior. Chapter 1, "A Technology of Behavior", p. 11, describes the influence of genetic endowment on behavior.

  - — (1974) *About Behaviorism*, Chapter 14, "Summing Up", pp. 226–229, provides the rationale for the study of animals as a stage in the experimental analysis of behavior. Chapter 1, "Causes of Behavior", pp. 9–20, sets forth Skinner's basic position as well as critiques of other points of view. Chapter 8, "Causes and Reasons", pp. 119–136, deals with approaches people use in the analysis of their behavior.

3 Wheeler attempts to account for this point with his organismic laws.

4 One wonders about extreme examples of such seemingly spontaneous change.

mined by our genetic and personal history.[5] I assume that. I can't prove it, but it is a working assumption.

History is full of conversions; St Paul on the road to Damascus; St Peter at the proclamation of his destiny by Jesus; Gauguin in his change of career. G.H. Mead, the American pragmatist, accounts for the phenomenon of sudden capriciousness in his concept of the "dynamic I". See Note 5 following.

5 This principle anticipates *Beyond Freedom and Dignity* as well as his conception of himself as the twentieth century behavioral Darwin. It seems that with his apparent denial of "will", Skinner's only explanation for capricious (idiosyncratic) behavior is that such behavior has been latent in the totality of the organism's contingency conditions. In conversation, Skinner confirmed no "freedom" and no "dignity". In other words, the organism could not possibly have self determined (willed) an idiosyncratic departure, but with careful examination of his/her repertoires of response it might have theoretically been anticipated. It would seem that the condition of totality of response repertoires is not random, but rather, chaotic in the meaning suggested in chaos theory, Glick (1988), *Chaos*; that is, containing a deeply patterned regularity. If sufficient data of the totality of stimulus/response condition could be programmed, the seeming idiosyncrasy of behavioral response would be exposed as complexly patterned rather than capricious.

G.H. Mead (1937), while essentially behaviorist, allowed for the phenomenological behavioral exception of idiosyncrasy in his concept of the "dynamic I", existing as a place holding exception in the more regularised condition of the (objective) "me" which he describes as the historical sum total of behavioral responses in an organism's past. That is, the objective "me" is the totality of the individual's identity until any given instant. The dynamic "I" is the potential the individual possesses to behave in the next instant in a manner not predictable on the basis of past behavior.

• — B.F. Skinner (1953), *Science and Human Behavior*, Chapter III, "Why Organisms Behave", pp. 26–27, describes the role of heredity in behavior.

• — (1938), *The Behavior of Organisms*, Chapter 13, "Conclusions", pp. 441–442, indicates that the importance of a "science of behavior derives largely from the possibility of an eventual extension to human affairs," but urges caution relative to allowing "questions of ultimate application to influence the development of a systematic science at an early stage." Chapter 1, p. 6, "A System of Behavior" provides a definition of behavior.

• — (1948), *Walden II*, Chapter 11, pp. 89–92, is an exposition of the role of environment and family history in the development of musical ability.

• — (1957), *Verbal Behavior*, pp. 462–464, provides a commentary on the relationship between animal cries and verbal behavior.

R.W.H.   Is it that you are primarily interested in stimuli and responses and you are not interested in some things that you can't observe that go on between the time of the stimulus and the response?

B.F.S.   Well, that is not quite right. I am interested in everything that I can find anything out about in so far as it bears on human behavior. I do, at the moment, neglect the inside of the organism in the sense of the nervous system and the rest of the internal mechanisms not because I think they are not important,[6] I am sure they are, but because you can't do

---

6   If the interview had been done in 1995, rather than in 1959 neurophysiologists would have had much more to say about the brain. Whether or not the enormous amount of new data from the interdisciplinary field of neuroscience would have influenced Skinner's thinking is doubtful.
   By 1989, beset with attacks on behaviourism by the dreaded enemy, cognitive psychology, Skinner fought back.

> The battle cry of the cognitive revolution is "Mind is back!" A "great new science of mind" is born. Behaviorism nearly destroyed our concern for it, but behaviorism has been overtyhrown, and we can take up again where the philosophers and early psychologists left off.
>
> Extraordinary things have certainly been said about the mind. The finest achievements of the species have been attributed to it; it is said to work at miraculous speeds in miraculous ways. But what it is and what it does are still far from clear. The mind that has made its comeback is not the mind of Locke or Berkeley or of Wundt or William James. We do not observe it; we infer it. We do not see ourselves processing information, for example. We see the materials that we process and the product, but not the producing. We now treat mental processes like intelligence, personality, or character traits – as things no one ever claims to see through introspection. Whether or not the cognitive revolution has restored mind as the proper subject matter of psychology, it has not restored introspection as the proper way of looking at it. The behaviorists' attack on introspection has been devastating.
>
> Cognitive psychologists have, therefore, turned to brain science and computer science to confirm their theories. Brain science, they say, will eventually tell us what cognitive processes really are. They will answer, once and for all, the old questions about monism, dualism, and interactionism. By building machines that do what people do, computer science will demonstrate how the mind works.
>
> What is wrong with all this is not what philosophers, psychologists, brain scientists, and computer scientists have found or will find; the error

much about them at the moment, especially in the living and intact organism in which you are interested. You can't go into a school and twist the neurons around in the brain of a child, and until you can, I am not very

---

is the direction in which they are looking. No account of what is happening inside the human body, no matter how complete, will explain the origins of human behavior. What happens inside the body is not a beginning. By looking at how a clock is built, we can explain why it keeps good time, but not why keeping time is important, or how the clock came to be built that way. We must ask the same questions about a person. Why do people do what they do, and why do the bodies that do it have the structures they have? We can trace a small part of human behavior, and a much larger part of the behavior of other species, to natural selection and the evolution of the species, but the greater part of human behavior must be traced to contingencies of reinforcement, especially to the very complex social contingencies we call cultures. Only when we take those histories into account can we explain why people behave as they do.

Skinner (1989), pp. 22–24

Williams Lyons (1995) offers a review of the last 100 years of philosophy of mind. It provided a useful review (or introduction) to concepts of mental function. There are, of course, many popular books on modern psychology of the brain, such as Colin Blakemore's *The Brain Machine* (1988).

Edelman and Mountcastle (1988), describe a theory which could possibly explain human consciousness. Their research indicates that the brain contains many more nerve cells than had previously been believed, some 50 billion. Those nerve cells within the neocortex are arranged in mini columns that are grouped into macrocolumns. Some of these columns receive primary sensory input from lower brain areas while many others receive their input from those columns that themselves receive the primary input. Furthermore, it appears that these secondary columns performing integrating functions exist at several levels within the highest brain functions occurring in those columns located furthest from the primary sensory input. These secondary columns seem to perform integrative functions.

Considerable degeneracy exists with respect to the neuronal interconnections and the specific neurons within columns that handle the incoming information. It appears that more than one arrangement is capable of performing the same function which accounts for the ability of some individuals to relearn tasks lost following brain injury or disease.

In addition, the integrative functions appear to rely heavily upon a re-entrant arrangement of processed nerve impulses. In other words, signals at any given level are returned to the next lower level as well as being sent to higher

much interested in that. I have no doubt that when I teach a child something today and discover that he knows it tomorrow, in the sense behaves in a different way tomorrow, that something survived overnight inside the child.

Now, I don't think for a moment that what survived was a mental memory. That I think is an outmoded concept we can do without[7], but what did survive is a changed child, a changed organism, partly in the brain and, I suppose, other parts of the body may have been different as a result of what happened to him yesterday. We have that different child[8] here today and we observed his behavior and we say, yes, he still knows what we taught him yesterday.

If I saw any chance of making use of that storage mechanism, I would look into it, but I can't. All I can do is to put something in today and predict that it will be there tomorrow and I can do that in the light of my past experiments.

R.W.H.   Yes, sir, and obviously you are retaining the possibility that there is much that you don't know and maybe can't know and work scientifically.

B.F.S.   Oh, absolutely, and as soon as the neurologist and the physiologists and the psychophysiologist get around to all this to give us some way

---

integrative centers. This re-entrant function is responsible for enhancing or inhibiting the processing of further signals and appears to be at the very heart of the learning process.

Consciousness, then, results in or from the highest integrative functions essentially integrating past experience with present inputs to form sharp distinctions of self and non self.

7   In that Skinner sees psychology as the science of behavior, it is change in behavior in which he is interested, not "mind". One is reminded of Bishop Berkeley's elimination of "matter" in his construct of immaterialism. Matter is a product of individual perception. There is no need of a concept of an objective layer of reality called matter. Neither is there for Skinner need of a concept of objective reality called "mind", wherein are contained mental memories. Between Berkeley and Skinner we are able to eliminate both mind and matter.

8   Not only is learning "change in behavior". To Skinner learning is "changed organism". This means change in any domain of behavior; cognitive, affective or psychomotive.

of observing what is going on at the time we want to know about it, I will be very happy to have all of that information.[9]

What I have always objected to is what I call the conceptual nervous system. A nervous system that you infer. When someone says, "Of, I feel terrible, my nerves are on edge", well, no one ever saw a nerve on edge. They don't have edges, but that is a useful idiom perhaps to suggest that something inside you is "pointed up" and a "little sharp" and "rasping", but actually it doesn't help and in the long run hinders a careful description of behavior to appeal to these "phony" nervous systems.[10]

---

9   It is obvious that since the time of this early interview cognitive psychology has become a focus of intense interest and scrutiny. While it may be true that brain physiology and extensive research activity in the field of artificial intelligence may have rendered the idea of consciousness or introspection moot, educators are still unable to "twist the neurons around in the brain of a child." The concept of "mind" was inimical to Skinner at the time of this interview and was doubtless so until the end of his life. ("Show me a mind!" he remarked.) Yet, the thought in 1959 and obviously more so today is that there are interventions – pharmacological, physiological and perhaps psychological which effect brain function and interdict conditioning in the relationship between stimulus and response.

- Skinner (1953). For an expanded discussion of the issues raised, see pp. 27–35 related to "inner causes" of the behavior of organisms.
- — *Contingencies of Reinforcement*, (1969), Chapter 9, "The Inside Story", pp. 280–284, deals with a consideration of the nervous system as an unproductive path to the study of human behavior.
- — (1971), Chapter 1, "A Technology of Behavior", pp. 11–15, discusses the pitfalls of attributing human behavior to non observable phenomenon rather than undertaking a scientific analysis of behavior.
- — (1974), Chapter 13, "What is Inside the Skin?", pp. 217–218, gives consideration to the conceptual nervous system. Chapter 5, "Perceiving", pp. 82–84, discusses remembering. Chapter 7, "Thinking", pp. 109–110, treats techniques of recall and memory storage.
- — *Upon Further Reflections*, (1987), Chapter 7, "Cognitive Science and Behaviorism", pp. 100–101, provides a criticism of the "storage" concept as an explanation for behavior change.
- Buckminster Fuller (1981) *Critical Path*, had some objections to metaphors such as the sun "rising" as it distorts the reality of points on the earth rotating into the sun's light.

10 • B.F. Skinner (1938), Chapter 1, "A System of Behavior", p. 3, provides brief references to the "nervous system as a fictional explanation of behavior". Chapter 12, "Behavior and the Nervous System", pp. 418–432, demonstrates

R.W.H. Critics of you and other experimental psychologists have always complained that research on "lower form" organisms cannot, simply and directly, extend to human organisms. Some critics claim your work cannot have meaning for education and that you might not even care. Obviously this is false.

B.F.S. Well, I think it is false. I don't know what "meaning for education" can mean in itself, but I am concerned with bringing about the changes in people which educators are supposed to bring about. I don't believe that this is at all helpful to say that when you teach a child you "broaden his mind" or "train his mental faculties" or any such things. Those are phrases that go very well at commencement addresses, but they don't give you any hint as to how you can go about improving the instructional process.[11]

Nobody has ever worked out a better way of "training the reasoning power". There just isn't any such thing. It is just a figure of speech used to describe certain conditions and behaviors. And if you define the goals of education in terms of the behavior, then you can see what sorts of methods are likely to help you get to those goals.[12]

---

the independence of the science of behavior from neurology which the author asserts must be established as a separate discipline.

- — *Reflections on Behaviorism and Society* (1978), Chapter 9, "The Experimental Analysis of Behavior (A History)", p. 123 – comments on the nervous system; p. 76 – Memory; p. 81, discusses the relation of study of organism over the environment. Chapter 4, "Humanism and Behaviorism", pp. 49–50, comments on introspection and internal mechanisms; Chapter 8, "Why I am Not a Cognitive Psychologist", p.110, gives consideration to cognitive processes and physiology.

11 An interviewer said to Skinner, "I think I have a definition of mind that you could accept. Mind is the sum total of all the macro and micro stimulus-response phenomena in an organism's experience." He said, "Maybe."

12 There is a certain irony in the image that has often been held of Skinner as a deterministic ogre seeking to manipulate organisms to his will. Paradoxically, there is a certain almost naïve optimism about the man and his position. What he is saying here is that the organism is currently behaving "x". Given due consideration (involving the possibility of mutual values determinations) it might be "better" if it/he/she behaved "y". What interventions might bring about this change? Accepting the existence of certain predispositions Skinner posits a way. Nowhere does he "write off" organisms dismissively.

- B.F. Skinner (1953), p.38. The author explains the rationale for study of

R.W.H. Education, then, is change in behavior.

B.F.S. That is all it is and that is all it has ever been.[13]

R.W.H. Yes. What are the implications for individual differences in this? How do individuals differ at birth? How do you feel about individual differences? Is it as Thorndike[14] thought that it has something to do with complexity of the nervous system? What are the individual differences based on then?

---

animal behavior; re: its advantages. Chapter XXVI, "Education", pp. 402–412, emphasises techniques of control and resulting behaviors.

* — (1968), Chapter 5, "Why Teachers Fail", pp. 110–113, reveals Skinner's view of the concept of the goal of developing rational power.
* — (1974), Chapter 11, "The Self and Others", p. 184, treats the impact of "mentalistic theories" of learning on education.

13 There. He said it. Skinner plain and simple. Would he likewise say that "*learning* is change in behavior?" It is the view of the interviewer that he would, and that, thus, education is to be equated with learning. The simple statement is loaded, for he means *all* behaviors, simple to complex; i.e. behaviors of skills, knowledge, understandings, attitudes and feelings. It is the position of the interviewer that Skinner's acquiescence to the fact that education is change in behavior may or not assume the necessity of the *integration* of behaviors, that is the *processing* of new behavior acquisition, in that processing involves new behaviors, but matters become extremely complicated.

* B.F. Skinner (1971), Chapter 4, "Alternatives to Punishment", pp. 91–97, discusses the process of changing behavior by "changing a mind".
* — (1978), Chapter 2, "Are We Free to Have a Future?", p. 16, discusses the extension of the study of animal behavior to humans, brief comment.
* — (1987), Chapter 2, "What is Wrong with Daily Life in the Western World", p. 28, defines the task of education.

14 The reference is to the early 20th century educational psychologist, Edward Lee Thorndike (1931), who viewed the organism as being like an old fashioned telephone switchboard with many potential circuits or very few. If there were many and they weren't "exercised", they might as well not exist. If there were few circuits and they were well "exercised", the organism might behave at a higher level of functioning than the one with under exercised circuits.

* B.F. Skinner (1953), p. 75 discusses individual differences.
* — (1948), pp. 195–199, provides a brief introduction to concepts of differences in variables and differences in processes.
* — (1948), Chapter 15, pp. 126–127, accounts for the phenomenon of individual differences.

B.F.S.   Well, individual differences are observable facts and they are not explained by saying that the brains differ. No one has ever shown any correlation between behavioral property and a neurological one which would explain the so-called individual differences of an intellect or traits of character.[15] I am sure that we are all born with very different endowments. Some are capable of very high development and some are probably not.

The only difference that turns up in work and teaching seems to be a difference in the speed with which people can acquire new behavior and how well they hold it.[16] In some cases it slips away. They can acquire it, but they lost it too fast and are never able to build up a very complicated repertoire of responses. Others are.

- — (1969), Chapter 5, "Operant Behavior", pp. 105–108, discusses Thorndike's Law of Effect. Further comment can be found in Chapter 5, "An Operant Analysis of Problem Solving", pp. 133–135.
- — (1974), Chapter 4, "Operant Behavior", p. 48, provides brief reference to Thorndike's "Law of Effect".
- — (1978), Chapter 3, "The Ethics of Helping People", pp. 35–36, and Chapter 9, "The Experimental Analysis of Behavior (A History)", pp. 115–116, discuss Thorndike's "Law of Effect".
15 The interviewers do not know this to be a fact. Cognitive psychology is concerned with this, of course.
- B.F. Skinner (1974), Chapter 10, "The Inner World of Motivations and Emotions", pp. 149–150, discusses genetic endowment and personality. Chapter 14, "Summing Up", pp. 224–225 and pp. 241–242 discuss individual uniqueness.
16 This would appear to provide Skinner's concept of "intelligence", that is, that intelligence resides in the ability of the organism to change behavior (learn) quickly and in its ability to retain that change long enough to have it effect subsequent behavior. This account satisfies the writers as a raw definition, but raises questions of context. Context seems a neutral enough condition which might include the notions of "motivation", "process emergence", "developmental readiness", "closure", and other such nomenclature favoured by some gestaltists.

   One is reminded of the often cited example of a weak, small statured, passive mother who incredibly finds the strength and will to lift a motor car off her trapped child single-handedly. The mother under normal circumstances might be mentally or physically incapable of action, but in the context of a specific emergency, behaves in an extraordinary manner.
- B.F. Skinner (1980), p.328. Skinner speculates about innate behavior.
- — (1987), Chapter 14, "Some Thoughts About the Future", pp. 203–204, draws the relationship between intelligence and reaction time.

R.W.H.   But you wouldn't hazard a guess as to why this might be?

B.F.S.   Well, I know perfectly well that many so-called differences are just due to bad education or a bad environmental history as I don't take any stock in the so-called "mathematical mind" notion. I think that a student by the sixth grade decided if he hasn't got a "mathematical mind" just missed out in some stage of the development and if he had been properly taught he might very well be just as good as everybody else in the class.[17]

R.W.H.   Conditioning at home would certainly be a factor in that.

---

17 This represents another example of optimism in Skinner's view. He obviously believed that any "normal" child could potentially learn anything within broad parameters of predisposition. It is somewhat remindful of Jerome Bruner's (1961) *The Process of Education* maxim that one could teach anything to anybody at any time at some level of sophistication, and that the learning could be reinforced at successive levels of sophistication through the process of education.

It is further optimistic in that it suggests that, technically at least, it's never too late to make "repairs" in a flawed experience, that the flaw is in the experience and not in the organism. Once again he is not dismissive of the student as permanently and irrevocatively "damaged goods".

One is reminded that if his definition of intelligence is true it does not mean that because a student doesn't learn algebra on cue, that is, at a fixed rate in a fixed time, as in most mathematics classes, that such a student is destined to a determined social class, occupational status, intellectual functioning. Skinner no doubt believed that schools were not places where students could be taught and learn, but, rather, ineffectual social inventions where what teachers knew best was *selection* in a process of educational Darwinism.

- B.F. Skinner (1968), Chapter 4, "The Technology of Teaching", p.56, addresses the questions of differences in study ability accommodated by teaching machines. Chapter 11, "Behavior of the Establishment", pp. 240–242, discusses the provision for accommodation of a wide range of differences among students.
- — (1978), Chapter 12, "Designing Higher Education", pp. 135–136, considers individual learning pace.

B.F.S.   Or he could have been out of school at a critical time when something was taken up and in our present system if a child falls behind, he stays behind.[18]

R.W.H. We recognise that much of your work is of a technical nature and yet in much of your terminology there is the suggestion of concepts which have a relationship to teaching and learning. You speak of intensity of stimulus, retention, rate of response, reinforcement and reflex reserve. How do these terms relate to one another?

B.F.S.   Well, those are rather technical concepts. The notion of reflex reserve was the very temporary phase in my thinking. I rejected it a year after I published it.

Although people like to argue about theories and systems and have kept the thing going for twenty or more years, but actually it was just an attempt to state the momentary condition of an organism which would enable you to predict what it will do with an extinction curve. You build up certain predispositions to behave and that you can predict under certain circumstances this behavior will come out without any further reward or reinforcement, but it turned out to be a quite useless concept because we discovered that the number of responses made in extinction is not independent of the deprivation level, motivational level, as I thought it was at the time I set up that concept. That is not a useful term at all. It is my one little excursion into theory and fully justifies my opinion of theories.[19]

---

18 Skinner seems to ignore the notion of maturational readiness. Could it not be possible that although the teacher *did* teach the mathematical concept and most children in the class were maturationally ready, some were out of synchronization with the others or could not grasp a key concept. Three months later or one week later the child might have easily acquired it. Another, perhaps more complicated problem might be that children who are not taught concepts when they are maturationally ready have even greater difficulty integrating material acquired later than might be sequentially appropriate. Maturational readiness is a key element in Wheeler's conception, a consideration Wheeler calls "pace".

19 One calls to mind an image of graduate students studying far into the night mastering Skinner's theory of reflex reserve. It is interesting to remember that early on in his life, Skinner aspired to become a novelist. He did, of course,

As to the other sort of thing, the notion of the rate of response was just a way of getting a probability of response and what you want to do is to be able to predict how likely it is that an organism will behave in a given way. Or what is the probability of his behavior and what we study are all of those things which will push that probability around, will make the organism more likely or less likely to do this.

The best way to show this is to just to give him a free situation and see how rapidly he will engage this behavior.

R.W.H. Yes, the rate of response has a time implication.

B.F.S. There is the situation in which the response can be freely repeated and is so. In our experiments we may get rates ranging from one response every few minutes to many thousands per hour. Certainly they vary by a factor of 3,000 to 1, a range over which rates can vary. We have all sorts of very subtle ways of pushing up to very high rates or holding an organism to very low steady rates and changing the rates back and forth. This is not awfully important in the application to education. The schedules which will generate high rates can be used to generate not so much mere rates, because the student isn't repeating something again and again, but what you would call interest or zeal or enthusiasm.

We can build schedules into our programs that create a highly dedicated type of scholar or scientist. It is this tendency to be very active which is one of the goals of good teaching.[20]

---

with *Walden II* and gave that up with finality. His departure from theory seems less resolved, as much of his later work seems an attempt at grand theory.

• B.F. Skinner (1938), Chapter 1, "A System of Behavior", pp. 26–27, provides discussion of reflex reserve as a "convenient way of representing the particular relation that obtains between the activity of a reflex and its subsequent strength."

20 It was certainly important among the great educational theorists of the progressive movement. John Dewey sought after an active learning process. It would be interesting to compare the *self* generative action desired by Dewey with the seeming *other* generative action achieved in behavioral theory. Of course Skinner would define out "self generated" in that behavior is "other generated", in that its continuity is a product of reinforcement contingencies.

• Skinner (1938), Chapter 1, "A System of Behavior", pp. 19–21, discusses the distinction between operant and respondent behavior. Chapter 6, "Some Functions of Stimuli", pp. 261–262, discusses the overlap of Operant and Re-

R.W.H.   And so, then, this ties in with what people speak of a motivation which is a word that you don't use.

B.F.S.   Well, I would use it in connection with deprivation, but I don't think we any longer deprive children.[21]

At one time in an English school system, the children were badly underfed and you could use a cookie to reinforce them, but we don't have

---

spondent – a somewhat technical commentary on the phenomenon.

*   — (1968), Chapter 7, "The Motivation of the Student", discusses the creation of a dedicated student, pp. 162–165, though the utilization of "well-designed contingencies of reinforcement."

*   — (1969), Chapter 5, "Operant Behavior", pp. 105–132, provides a fully developed exposition of Skinner's view of this behavior. "Preface", pp. vii–xii, Skinner describes his view of theory as well as the kind of theory necessary for scientific analysis of behavior.

*   — (1971), Chapter 1, "A Technology of Behavior", pp. 17–18, discusses the shaping of behavior by consequences. Chapter 8, "The Design of a Culture", pp. 156–158, presents material about the design of educational environments.

*   — (1974), Chapter 3, "Operant Behavior", pp. 46–71, treats the issues raised in this segment except for that of reflex reserve, a construct which Skinner had already abandoned at the time of the interview. The chapter provides an introduction to the topic which should be most helpful to teachers seeking information about the concept. Ratio of responses and reinforcement is discussed on pp. 59–60 of Chapter 3.

*   — (1978), Chapter 4, "The Experimental Analysis of Behavior (A History)", pp. 119–120, Operant Behavior. Chapter 3, "The Ethics of Helping People", pp. 35–36, discusses probability of occurrence of behavior. Chapter 2, "Are We Free to have a Future?", pp. 19–21, describes operant and respondent conditioning. Chapter 14, "The Force of Coincidence", pp. 171–175, reviews operant conditioning, coincidence and superstition.

*   — (1987), Chapter 4, "Selection by Consequences", p. 52, describes operant conditioning as a kind of selection by consequences. Chapter 5, "Evolution of Behavior", pp. 72–73, discusses the evolution of operant conditioning. Chapter 2, "What is Wrong with the Western World", pp. 17–19 discusses operant reinforcement within a social context.

21 B.F. Skinner obviously had not spent much time in schools. Children are deprived in any number of ways. Most importantly, they can be deprived of self esteem. They are often deprived of freedom and dignity, which Skinner admits exist for some in the domain of "feeling", if not in his behavioral reality.

*   — (1953), Chapter IX, examines "deprivation and satiation", pp. 141–159.

undernourished children that we can use rewards within that sense. We don't deliberately starve children so that food will be more important to them or anything like that.[22] We do, of course, use punishment and make them more intense to generate escape, but that is a technique that I don't approve of either.[23] The point I think you are making is perfectly correct that which a moderate kind of motivation, that is where the individual separate reward isn't very important if you schedule it the right way it becomes very important. You can build up. For example, gambling devices contain a schedule of reinforcement called variable ratio schedule, and if you have ever been to a bingo game or Las Vegas you know what effect this has on human behavior. It generates extremely high rates of activity.[24]

---

22 It would be difficult to say "nothing like that". While the interviewer was a visitor to schools for travelling children in Northern Ireland, 1970–77, teachers deprived children from baths which they delighted in and reinforcing desired behavior by appropriately providing baths. Certainly hundreds of thousands of children in schools everywhere live in a state of physical and emotional deprivation every day of their lives. Contingencies of reinforcement are seldom arranged so that such children's lives are improved.

23 He is, of course, describing aversive punishment which, in effect, is negative reinforcement. The reinforcement is in fact that it feels so good when punishment ceases. Such a programme can effectively *prevent* behaviour but seldom is generative of positive behavioral change. It prevents. It does not produce.

• B.F. Skinner (1953), Chapter XII, examines "punishment", pp. 182–193.

• — (1959), Part II, pp. 131–141, looks at "Reinforcement Today".

• — (1968), Chapter 5, "Why Teachers Fail", note pp. 95–104 which treat the use of aversive behavioral control within the brief commentary on the movement away from aversive practices in Western culture as a whole. Chapter 9, "Discipline, Ethical Behavior and Self Control", pp. 185–191, contains a discussion of punishment. Chapter 10, "A Review of Teaching", pp. 199–126, contains the most useful material related to learning and reinforcement. The concept, an integral part of the entire book, is well illuminated in this chapter.

• — (1971), Chapter 4, "Punishment", pp. 68–82, provides an exposition of issues related to punitive control and the concept of responsibility as it relates to punishment and goodness.

• — (1974). In addition to Chapter 4, "Operant Behavior", already cited, Chapter 10, "The Inner World of Motivation and Emotion", focuses on the "uselessness" of relying on "inner causes" as an explanation of motivation.

24 Local carnival hustlers are past masters of this. A favorite is to provide generously sized rings which can easily be hooped over clothes pegs standing erect in the booth. The operator removes the hooped clothes peg and shows

A crooked gambler knows this. He knows how to build up his victim by letting him win on a variable ratio schedule until his victim has extraordinary confidence he is going to keep on winning and then the phony deck is slipped in and the gambler "takes him" during a long process of extinction during which the victim plays again, and again loses all his money.

Or, for example, a newspaper puzzle contest, advertising contest, always begins with very easy puzzles, building it up more and more difficult until the very end. If it is an expensive contest, you will have your public libraries jammed with people in their research in the reference rooms late at night working like mad to finish that final puzzle. Well, now, that's a spectacle that your college librarian never sees.[25]

---

the player one side of the pin displaying a "winning" number. One must hoop three winning numbers to win the big prize. He/she quickly is shown two "winning" numbers at fifty pence per play, the third winning number is never shown. The operator palms the pin to show the reverse side displaying all losing numbers. Needless to say, successive losing numbers are shown to the player who is hypnotised by the big prize as he/she loses continuously until the playing behavior is extinguished or all of his/her money is spent. The operator then generously provides the disappointed punter with a cheap balloon or a plastic coin as a consolation prize.

- — (1957) *Schedules of Reinforcement*. Primarily a report of work performed under contract to the Office of Naval Research and with Harvard University between 1949 and 1955, this work is of special interest to the professional psychologist. It provides no interpretation of data collected from experiments utilizing birds and human subjects. The material, however, is not without interest to the professional educator as ... "The primary purpose of the present book is to present a series of experiments designed to evaluate the extent to which the organism's own behavior enters into a determination of its subsequent behavior. From a formulation of such results we should be able to predict the effect of any schedule." (p. 3)

  Further, Ferster and Skinner state that "In research in psychophysics, problem solving and motor skills, lower organisms may now be used as conveniently as human subjects and with many advantages arising from the greater possibility of many types of control. Performances generated by particular schedules have proved to be useful in the study of motivation (e.g. in the analysis of ingestive and sexual behavior), of emotion (e.g. in the study of "anxiety"), of punishment, of escape and avoidance behavior, and effects of drugs." (p. 3)

25 The reason being that studying for examinations is related to negative reinforcement. There is seldom, if ever, positive reinforcement scheduled to gen-

R.W.H. No.

B.F.S. And yet it is perfectly within reach of education if you schedule successes properly there is no reason why not only the occasional student, but every student, would not be fired with a burning zeal to keep in there plugging.

R.W.H. There have got to be very meaningful rewards.

B.F.S. They have got to be frequent and they've got to be meaningful and they've got to be properly scheduled. You don't throw a big hurdle at the student or throw him at a big hurdle, I suppose would be better. You let him go over the hurdles, but the hurdles get higher and higher in a very carefully arranged series. And then his skill and pieces as he needs it and he remains successful.[26]

---

erate the learning activity. Activity in college libraries usually involves rising to skip out for coffee, falling asleep, yawning, whispering to neighbors and, in the days before biros, sharpening mostly unused pencils.
- — (1969), Chapter 5, pp. 125–127 and Chapter 6, pp. 159–160, contain useful material related to contingency shaped behavior which can be found in Note 5.1, Chapter 5, as well as in Note 6.2, Chapter 6. Chapter 5, "Operant Behavior", pp. 117–119, relates gambling and schedule of reinforcement. Chapter 67, "An Operant Analysis of Problem Solving", Note 6.3, includes the topic some kinds of rules, pp. 162–166.
- — (1971), Chapter 2, "Freedom" provides a discussion of a number of issues raised in this segment of the interview. Of particular interest are pp. 26–33 relative to reinforcers and p.35 relative to gambling.
- — (1974). Reinforcement schedules, variable-ration schedules of which gambling systems are examples are treated on pp. 57–61 in Chapter 4, as are punishment and negative reinforcement on pp. 61–64.
26 This describes the characteristics of operant conditioning. The steps between behavior A, the behavior to be extinguished (i.e. the state of unknowing or skilllessness), and behavior B, the behavior to be learned (i.e. the state of knowing or skilfulness), are divided into small steps. Each step is small enough that the student nearly always succeeds in getting the right answer. He/she is *immediately positively* reinforced implicitly by getting it right, or explicitly with a word, "Good boy/girl", or a token reward, candy or a five pound note. In particular difficult cases the reward must be particularly meaningful, i.e. something genuinely pleasurable to the student. In such examples a perceptive attempt must be made to discover the powerful reinforcer. In one ex-

R.W.H.   The teacher has got to be kind of a role player in all of this.

B.F.S.   Yes, except that actually this eventually breaks down and the teacher cannot reinforce often enough and quickly enough to build the optimal schedules of reinforcement. That is where the machines come in. They are designed to apply to the human organism what we know about the most effective schedules of reinforcement.[27]

---

treme case with a seriously disturbed child, the charge agent found the reinforcer in allowing the boy to urinate out an open first floor window after each success. Obviously this was an extreme instance, but one person's reinforcer is another's pure indulgence. See Wheeler Interview, Note 12.

• — (1987), Chapter 11, "Can the Experimental Analysis of Behavior Rescue Psychology", pp. 165–169, encompasses a somewhat technical discussion of reinforcement and operant behavior. Chapter 14, "Some Thoughts about the Future", pp. 205–206, is a brief commentary on study of reinforcement utilizing pigeons.

27 In other words, while general reinforcement is always useful in generating behavioral change in students, individuals and groups, it is never easy. Teachers need to develop extensive and particularised schedules of group and individual reinforcement and extensive creative and particularised reinforcers. The task is daunting and eventually impossible. Skinner always advocated mechanical individualised aid, initially in the form of teaching machines commercially developed and programmed. In the early phase of this activity in the early 1960s publishers rushed to capitalise on what promised to be a revolution in the learning business. Programmed books and teaching machines, simple and complex, flooded the market. The push was short lived and by the end of the decade publishers had given up, frustrated by the difficulty in developing programmes, some said individuals who were sophisticated enough in the content, were totally disinterested in engaging themselves in the development of operant minutiae.

The coming of the computer age has provided the technical means of overcoming many of the initial difficulties. Interactive computer programs have been moderately successful as long as the machines are maintained, the programmes updated and training for teachers is provided. Skinner was totally frustrated in his attempts to develop teaching machines commercially. He describes the saga in his autobiography, Skinner (1983), *A Matter of Consequences*, pp. 138–139, 258–260, 294–295. He was disenchanted dealing with the business interests and blamed the education establishment for an unwillingness to change. No revolution has occurred although a generation of young people have grown up conditioned by computer games to readiness for machine learning. The phenomenon of concentrated absorption of children

R.W.H. Now, in the machines, what is the reward to the student? Is it the fact that he gets this right or is it the fact that he is working with something mechanical? What are the rewards as you see them?

---

in mechanical devices recognised and described years ago by McLuhan (1964), overcomes problems of alleged short attention span (interest) and readies the child (person) for extended interaction with academic content before television monitors. With no acknowledgement to or recognition of Skinner, a *Time* magazine article, "Babes in Byteland", describes the flood of activity in the updated version of teaching machines.

Nearly two decades after the birth of personal computers, millions of techno-shy Americans are finally discovering a reason to bring them home. Filled with hope that their children will find learning as compelling as blasting aliens in a video game, parents bought more than $243 million worth of educational software last year, a 66% increase over 1992. The Popularity of kidware has made it not only the hottest segment of the $6.8 billion software industry but also a driving force behind the rapid growth in hardware sales. There are more than 15 million U.S. homes with both personal computers and school-age children; that figure is expected to double by 1988. "More and more parents see computers as something essential for their children's education," says Jean Cho, a manager of learning programs for software giant Microsoft. Dozens of companies are rushing to cash in on the boom. "It's had a huge impact, especially in their writing," Breitstein says. "They don't even know they're improving their skills."

In schools that use programs designed for classrooms, the news has been encouraging as well. One notable success story comes from Oklahoma City, where district officials had been set to close Dunbar Elementary, a virtually all-black school in a low-income neighborhood, because student scores on the Iowa Test of Basic Skills failed to meet state standards. In an eleventh-hour effort to save the school, the district two years ago used federal money to buy a computer learning program called SuccessMaker, developed by the Computer Curriculum Corp. of Sunnyvale, California. The software allows individual students to advance at their own pace through reading, math and science lessons. After spending as much as an hour a day at their terminals, the students produced average test scores 50% higher than before; that helped persuade officials to keep the school open last year.

While home software tends to be more light-hearted than programs for schools, the two have many features in common. For example, students who log on to the classroom-oriented SuccessMaker instantly get a read-

B.F.S.   The getting it right and getting on to the next step. The pinball features of teaching machines aren't important at all. Small children may get a little fun out of operating a machine, that is incidental. The novelty wears off. The novelty of the material that is going through the machine remains because the student never knows what is coming off next. There is always just the slight possibility that he may be wrong, but the fact is that he is almost always right and he gallops ahead with a kind of delight in his work which is a great surprise to the average teacher.[28]

---

ing passage that, like home software, may include animation. A correct answer brings immediate affirmation, just as it does on a home computer – a response that not even the most attentive teacher in a classroom filled with 20 or 30 students can provide. Wrong answers are greeted with new lessons that reinforce the material. Students thus advance only when they are ready for new levels, sharply lowering the risk that individuals will fall behind the rest of the class as it marches ahead on a rigid schedule.

Jackson, 1994

It looks as if Skinner were right except for his notion of reducing distracting garish stimuli in reading materials. Skinner's failure to find successful entry into the marketplace with teaching machines simply meant that the technology was slightly behind his conception and that, in any event, the world of commerce always waits until they have clearly established control of monitoring release of a new technology and the means of preserving maximum financial benefit for themselves.

* B.F. Skinner (1948), Chapter 15, pp. 123–125, deals with motivation of learners and "fortifying" children against discouragement.
* — (1968), Chapter 7, "The Motivation of the Student", pp. 145–168 explains the concept of motivation with the context defined by Skinner. The chapter provides a base for an understanding of the utilization of the teaching machines as an aide to instruction.
* — (1987), Chapter 8, "The Shame of American Education", pp. 124–126, discusses reinforcement provided by programmed subject matter.

28 Here it is 1995, and there haven't been many surprised teachers in schools. He certainly was correct with respect to computers.

* B.F. Skinner (1969), Chapter 1, "The Role of the Environment", pp. 18–19, discusses employment and money, as a reinforcer.
* Skinner (1987), Chapter 3, "News from Nowhere, 1984", pp. 42–43, provides an update on schools in *Walden Two* between 1948 and 1984, including a brief note of development of computers and re-statement of Skinner's position.
* — (1987), Chapter 12, "The Contrived Reinforcer", pp. 175–179, discusses reinforcers within an educational and industrial setting.

R.W.H. The teacher in a classroom could not take advantage of operant possibilities without machine assistance, is that correct?

B.F.S. Yes, a teacher with a class of twenty or twenty-five students simply can't do this because she hasn't got the contact with the students. She is holding back the good students and she is forcing the slow, but the machine can do it, but, as you say, you have got to program this material very carefully and that is the thing we are working on right now to find how to program materials for maximal instruction.[29]

R.W.H. This is assuming in the beginning that the student has a desire to learn something of the data.

B.F.S. Oh, we are not assuming that. Of course, if you've got a student who has been badly riddled by existing aversive controls in school and very negative, and so on. I don't know what you might want to do to bring him around. A clinical psychologist, Dr Slack, here has been paying delinquent boys to come in for interviews and paying them for working on teaching machines and it might be necessary at times to overcome a negativism with something pretty explicit by way of reinforcement.[30]

---

29 While the interviewers would concede that with the right machine and the right program certain students would benefit by being painlessly led through conditioning to new behavior and new learning, one would need preliminary operant programs with explicit reinforcement to get them to even sit down to begin. It is not to say impossible, however. One need but look at the success of computer games with all types of children. Their addiction would seem to confirm Skinner's thesis. The fact that it has not been done yet does not say that it won't be done.

30 In this almost casual disengagement from a most critical concern, Skinner speaks of "badly riddled", "delinquent boys". He is dismissive in his sentence, "I don't know what you might want to do to bring him around." He then casually suggests that they might be rewarded by that most relevant, meaningful and explicit reinforcer of them all – money.

In personal conversation, Skinner warned the interviewers, who themselves had been deeply concerned with the educational problems of disaffected youth, to not get involved with complicated counselling and therapeutic approaches to dealing with them. Skinner urged the interviewers to ignore past histories and to get on with effecting specific behavioral change through the science of behavior. Extinguish the old, condition the new. It is, as all teachers know, easier said than done.

But our experience so far has been even in working in lower grade schools with this machine that after a certain period of timidity perhaps, or reticence, as soon as the child discovers that he can go forward, he does and will volunteer statements to the effect that, "Gee, if I had one of these I would be good at arithmetic!" He feels the change. Something is happening to him. There isn't any normal child who isn't reinforced by success. They have such small successes, ordinarily, in their school work.[31]

- B.F. Skinner (1959), Part III, *The Technology of Education*, "The Science of Learning and the Art of Teaching", pp. 145–157, which was first published in 1954, is a paper describing early work relating to the development of teaching machines. Skinner describes his thinking rooted in animal research and addresses the problem of developing a device which would provide students carefully designed instructional material as well as provide appropriate reinforcement, "Teaching Machines", pp. 158–182, discusses the development of teaching machines and, in particular, the process of programming material and level of difficulty of material. Illustrative material is included.

31 Skinner here presents a charming scene of life in a primary school probably not unlike his own had been in Western Pennsylvania early in the century. He describes the "gee whiz" ethos of American television, *Mr Roger's Neighborhood*. There still are individual classes in some schools wherein Skinner's brief scenario might be played. Children, such as the ones suggested here, are most often "self starters" under any circumstances and would find a way to learn if there were no teaching machines, teachers or schools for that matter.

   The interviewers would scarcely object to devices or techniques which would stimulate data acquisition and analysis. For example, if basic language mastery could be programmed within a semester or mathematics flaws could be repaired, fixed like a punctured bicycle tyre, with a branched programme in one day, or week or month, teachers would be thrilled.

   While the interviewers have no doubt that programmes could be anticipated that go beyond the data and into analysis and consideration of such data, they remain convinced that education is that which happens between teachers and learners after the "last fitful burp of the computer", Houghton (1967), pp. 53–63.

- B.F. Skinner (1978), Chapter 11, "The Free and Happy Student", pp. 140–148, deals broadly with the question of student motivation through "positive methods of education". Chapter 12, "Designing Higher Education", pp. 149–156, discusses the same topics. Chapter 10, "Some Implications of Making Education More Efficient", pp. 135–139, discusses programmed instruction, personalized instruction answering some objections to these instructional

R.W.H. We have so many kids in school who are seemingly "not normal". I am interested to hear you say about the clinical psychologist paying the young man. I know that a special school in Connecticut, a school for emotionally disturbed, they use money as a reward and punishment. They take the money, the allowance, away and this is really almost the only form of "punishment" they have.

B.F.S. Well, of course, what happens when you guarantee payment is that the money system works as a threatened punishment, not as a reward. But if you pay in terms of achievement, it can be very powerful.[32] It might much better be used that way. Quite a bit of work has been done in extrinsic reward systems; we have provisions for this machine to reinforce with either say gum drops or something like that or with tokens that could be exchanged for privileges. As extra dessert at lunch time or something like that. Once in a while the machine kicks one of these out for a right answer. That's quite a good possibility if you want to add it but I have regular faith in the human organism and I don't think it would be necessary.[33]

---

approaches. Chapter 12, "Designing Higher Education", pp. 156–159, discusses similar topics.

• — (1968). This text attempts to deal with the wide range of questions the student of education would bring to the utilization of the technology of the teaching machine. Of particular interest to teachers are the discussions relating to programming in Chapter 3, "Teaching Machines", pp. 39–53, as well as the material contained in Chapter 6, "Teaching Thinking", pp. 115–119, dealing with the designated topic. Chapter 3, "Teaching Machines", pp. 48–52, treats problems related to programming.

32 This is, of course, critical. The interviewers did not realize it at the time but the essence of Skinner's operant conditioning is to reinforce appropriate behaviors immediately and positively and in operants small enough to assure right responses. This is critically different from putting the promise of reward up front and reducing reward for wrong behaviors. This is what teachers often fail to recognize. The contingencies in most classrooms are almost deliberately rigged for failure, not success. Of course teachers would say it is almost impossible to arrange promising contingency conditions for some students in that *none* of their behaviors are "worthy" of reinforcement.

33 Skinner here reiterated his faith in the powerful intrinsic reinforcement, "getting it right". The interviewers do also. The difficulty is in providing infinite numbers of personalised programs which would be necessary to restore the "damaged" child, who is so used to "getting it wrong" that the prospect of

R.W.H.   Evaluation always in terms of observable behavior?

B.F.S.   Everything is in terms of observable behavior. You have no other information about people.[34]

R.W.H.   For example, in a regular school situation, how would you evaluate, how would you test? Would you test with the traditional teacher made tests of all kinds or do you thing those are valueless?

---

interfacing with any individual or device is an anathema.

Behavioral therapy has, of course, attempted and succeeded in many instances to de-program phobias. "I hate school" is a phobia all too common and, in many instances, testament to the child's sanity.

- B.F. Skinner (1987), Chapter 2, "What is Wrong with Daily Life in the Western World", pp. 18–26, examines the erosion of contingencies of reinforcement within the range of areas of human activity particularly within the workplace and government; pp. 27–31 address applied behavior analysis in education and in relation to other social problems. Chapter 7, "Cognitive Science and Behaviorism", pp. 109–110, contains brief commentary on teaching machines. Chapter 8, "The Shame of American Education", pp. 122–130, provides an approach to the solution of contemporary problems of education through the utilization of well-constructed teaching programs and the principles of Skinner's technological approach to education.

34 The interviewers do not agree with Skinner here. The interviewers believe that most behavior is value driven and that behavior, to give Skinner his due, is at the end of an operant series of "behavioral positions" that are, in the imagery of another metaphor, subliminal. That is, there are "behaviors", subliminal, but learned, that begin with a vague and undifferentiated awareness of a value, and proceed in a pattern of clarification and differentiation to a point of observable behavior as a manifestation of the original value. In this process, unobservable, but certain and necessary, there is movement through a series of subliminal operants reinforced deliberately or indeliberately toward observable manifestation. Great teachers sense (intuit) these movements and can deliberately reinforce them. They are like quarks, which had been known about by physicists *before* they had the instrumentation to observe that they had existed, if but momentarily. We know of the existence of such "subliminal" behaviors under current circumstances by being able to predict subsequent undifferentiated subliminal contingencies. Not only great teachers, but sensitive ordinary individuals engage in such interactions every day of their lives. The interviewers discussed this with Skinner. He did not disagree. Such micro behaviors, as yet unmonitorable by any available technology, no doubt exist. Body language, subtly manifested, is an example.

B.F.S.   How would I test whether the machines are working or not?

R.W.H.   No. How would you test or evaluate student performance in a regular classroom with or without machines? If then, education is change in behavior there may be something that you would be doing that would be seeking after specific behavioral change. How would you measure achievement in these other things? As you know, the tradition of assessment and/or evaluation are different in Europe and America. In the United States assessment is continuous. European education tends to postpone assessment and it becomes a terminal experience, in any case do you see ...

B.F.S.   I am not particularly interested in measurement. There are other people who could give you much better ideas about that. All tests come down to sampling behavior. Some of them sample it effectively and some of them don't. Actually with a machine we don't need tests. If the student gets through the material he has learned and there is no point in testing him and the grade he gets, if you still insist upon giving grades, they will simply tell you how far he has gone.

If you go all the way in the course, you get an A; if you go halfway through, you get a C, and if you want to take it next year and go all the way through and get an A, then that's the way it should be because you know it all then. The person who picked up an A would pick up another course the second year.[35]

---

35 Skinner here suggests the idea of non-graded school organisation, or perhaps a form of open education in which children proceed to "mastery" of content. Such plans are often "performance based" in which students demonstrate acquisition of goal determined objectives. Contemporary projects such as the essential school movement in the United States use teacher/pupil determined "demonstrations", exhibitions, portfolios and performances, to make manifest their learning (new behavior).

Most bureaucratic school organizations in the United States find such arrangements untidy, unwieldy, difficult to administer and bookkeep. They find it more manageable to rely on teacher assessment by means of teacher developed "tests" sometimes literally translated into "marks", traditionally A for excellent, B for good, C for fair, D for barely passing, and F, in red ink, for failure. Some European universities still measure graduate student performance in numerical percentages (82%, 74%, 51%) on written scripts. In addition, in the U.S. often under external pressure from school/government officials and the public, they administer commercially developed standardised "achievement" tests which are used normatively to compare individuals, classes,

R.W.H. Do I sense the implication that you are not in favor of this grading and marking?

B.F.S. Well, I think that if grades simply indicate what a student has accomplished, that they will be useful to educators in planning further work or employers, and so on, but if they are used simply to hold a sword of Damocles over the head of the students, what they are used for then, I'm entirely against them. Tests are ordinarily not given to find out what a student knows but what he doesn't know.[36] They want to make sure he gets back to that old text book again.

---

schools, school districts, states and national entities. In Ireland continuous assessment is rejected for such reasons as it would destroy the pupil-teacher relationship, it could never be fair and objective, parents might literally attack the teacher who assigned their child a "low" mark. Teacher unions object to assessment as not being part of a teacher's job. Assessment is then put off until the end of a period of instruction (the junior certificate, the leaving certificate). The results of such assessment literally determine the student's future life status.

Assessment of either U.S. or European method is far removed from Skinner's concept of do it 'til you get it right with no time constraints. His focus is on "learning", of course. Both the U.S. and the European assessment structures seem part of the educational selection procedure, the survival of the "educationally fittest".

- B.F. Skinner (1948), Chapter 15, pp. 118–120, discusses the lack of necessity for conventional grading.
- — (1974), Chapter 10, "The Inner World of Motivation and Emotion", pp. 159–160, contains a brief comment on mental measurement.
- — (1980), p. 98, "Assign and Test" sets out an informal note on teaching reading.

36 The interviewers strongly agree. Skinner is *not* simply being a soft altruistic fop. He knows that threat and punishment are outmoded concepts if one is seeking positive behavioral change. While intimidation will prevent behaviors, that will not be generative of positive behavioral change. This is not to say that behavioral control is not possible, but the random and generalized ethos of intimidation found in some schools merely creates an aura of unpleasantness. While sometimes cruel, it is seldom cruelly pointed enough to make children really "love Big Brother" as in Aldous Huxley's *Brave New World*.

- B.F. Skinner (1959), Part III, "Teaching Machines", p. 176, discusses student grading when utilizing teaching machines.
- — (1968), Chapter 3, "Teaching Machines", pp. 53–54, 100, describes student examinations as an aversive practice. Chapter 6, "Teaching Thinking",

R.W.H. We have talked about thoughts on behaviorism generally. How about the higher mental processes. Does behaviorism consider abstract thinking and seeing complicated relationships? Can we say just about the same things for these except that they are more complex.

B.F.S. That's right. No one has ever given a very good account of higher mental processes. Certainly not in terms of mental events or perceptual processes or anything else. I myself have been interested in analysis of verbal behavior[37] in these terms and I think it works as well as any at the present time. Any one of the things we are interested in here is teaching thinking. In our present behavioral formulation of that, and we're going to begin in the nursery school where we think we can really teach people to think clearly. And work there will be designed to teach children to observe carefully, to attend to details and not the details that have all been made garish and four colors and what not.

This whole effort to make text books challenging and interesting defeats the very purpose of education. The child never learns that the black and white page of print can be interesting. Nothing is interesting unless it has comic figures on it and we are definitely opposed to attracting the attention of the child because we want to teach him to pay attention.[38]

---

pp. 115–144, deals with many aspects of thinking including the issues raised in the interview.

• — (1978), Chapter 10, "Some Implications of Making Education More Efficient", p. 137, examinations in a personalized system of instruction are described briefly. Chapter 12, "Designing Higher Education", pp. 149–150, also discusses examinations.

37 Skinner (1978), Chapter 8, "Why I am Not a Cognitive Psychologist", pp. 108–112. Skinner (1982), Chapter 9, "A Lecture on Having a Poem", pp. 191–203.

38 Skinner was interested in children's learning to read. He attempted to attract the interviewers to engage in behavioral research in reading and was always agitated at the thought of attention draining garish illustrations in primers. Notice this last line of comment. Does he not mean "distracting attention", distracting from the child's task of "paying" attention to finding personal, meaningful response to regularised arrangement of alphabetic figures? It is supposed that authors and publishers fill children's' books with colorful illustrations to supplement the written text and to add to the child's total experience, hence, to sell more books. Skinner wants the contingencies arranged so that the "getting it right" in the child's written text is reinforcing. The publishers' assumption is "more is better". Skinner's assumption is reduce

R.W.H.   These are added stimuli which you want to remove.

B.F.S.   We want to get rid of that. We also want to teach a child to deliberate, not to react too quickly, to wait until he has evaluated the situation. We want to get him to re-arrange the material so that he has the best possible opportunity to come up with an appropriate response.

Now this should be carrying the same formulation right into logic, mathematics and scientific thinking.[39]

---

extraneous stimuli and control the contingencies. Educators often say, "How can we compete with media for the attention of the child? They are able to invest in hundreds of thousands of pounds to produce a one-minute advertising spot". There are two answers. The first is to control the contingencies. The second is to provide more effective reinforcers for desired behaviors. Begin by making the classroom an exciting, reinforcing of students mass action, places where children want to be. In Skinner's parlance, arrange the contingencies.

• B.F. Skinner (1969), Chapter 5, "Operant Behavior", pp. 116–117, discusses mental processes.

39 Skinner is certainly not alone in this desire to postpone response to stimuli. This paragraph is particularly interesting in light of the critics of Skinner accusations of thoughtlessness, mindlessness in operant process. G.H. Mead (1937) *Mind, Self, and Society*, defined "Mind" in terms of the ability to postpone response to stimuli. John Dewey's concept of intelligence is associated with internalised self discussion, of in-mind experimentalism where one "mentally" tries out possible solutions in problem solving activity. Dewey (1944), *Democracy and Education*, Chapter 25, "Theories of Knowledge", pp. 337–338, Dewey (1913), *Interest and Effort in Education*, Chapter IV, "Types of Educative Interest", pp. 83–84. One wonders what Skinner "thinks" is happening in this process of personal "evaluating". The interviewers apologise for not asking. All is not lost. Skinner abridges his conception of thinking in Skinner (1989), pp. 19–22.

• B.F. Skinner (1957), Chapter 19, pp. 432–452, treats the phenomenon of thinking with the limitations of the Skinnerian point of view. In Chapter 19 when discussing verbal behavior in relation to thinking, Skinner provides the following description of the process:

> This has been recognized traditionally when the behavior of a speaker with respect to himself as listener, particularly when his behavior is not observable by others, is set aside as a special human achievement called "thinking".

(p. 433)

R.W.H. Is there any relationship at all between behaviorism and the so called holistic theories of learning?

B.F.S. I don't see anything in field theory. Now that may be because I have not looked closely and someone has not taught me to look closely, but I have never felt they have done anything but name some problems and these problems are of interest to us, but their solutions are not because they tend not to be real solutions.

We can teach a child to observe, to attend to details, to organize materials and so on without falling back on essentially field principles. We do use something fairly close to it. For example, talk about the various kinds of repertoires that the organism may develop some of which approached continuous fields but we don't appeal to forces operating in these fields.[40]

In summary, he indicates that ... "as far as a science of behavior is concerned, Man Thinking is Simply Man Behaving." p. 452. The references cited above provide the context for Skinner's consideration of the topic. Chapter 5, pp. 107–114, for a consideration abstraction.

- — (1959), Part II, "Are Theories of Learning Necessary?", pp. 16–69, The area of "complex learning" is treated illustrated by such terms as "preferring", "choosing", "discriminating", "matching", "higher mental processes".
- — (1974), Chapter 6, "Verbal Behavior", pp. 93–94, considers abstraction and concepts. Chapter 7, "Thinking", pp. 102–118, explores the many aspects of the term thinking. Chapter 7, pp. 102–103. The term higher mental process is defined. Chapter 8, "Causes and Reasons", pp. 128–136, treat reason and reasoning, induction and deduction. Chapter 14, "Summing Up", p. 223, thinking, brief comment.
- — (1978), Chapter 4, "Humanism and Behaviorism", pp. 50–51, contrasts mental events, feelings. Chapter 8, "Why I am Not a Cognitive Psychologist", pp. 97–102, Skinner treats such terms as abstraction, idea, concept and mind within the context of his criticism of cognitive psychology.
- — (1980), p.136, "Reasoning defined."
- — (1987), Chapter 11, "Can the Experimental Analysis of Behavior Rescue Psychology?", pp. 161–163, presents a criticism of the concept, mind, held by cognitive psychologists.
40 The interviewers had in mind the work of Kurt Kofka, Wolfgang Kohler, Raymond H. Wheeler and Max Wertheimer. Skinner's reference to repertoires of response as perhaps having some relationship to the idea of continuous fields calls up Skinner's second example of "thought processes" in the previous note when he refers to imaging. "When we ... look at them."
- B.F. Skinner (1938), Chapter 13, "Conclusion", pp. 435–436, presents objections to Lewin's concepts of vectors and valences.

R.W.H.   I noticed that some people have made the assertion that Guthrie's work had implication for field theorists. I wondered how you felt about that.

B.F.S.   Well, I don't know and I wouldn't care.[41]

R.W.H.   I noticed in the card catalogue that you have a publication called *Walden Two*. I'm embarrassed to tell you that I haven't read it. I take it that it is a philosophical novel.

B.F.S.   Well, I don't know if it deserves that designation. It is a utopian novel. It is supposed to describe something which took place at an existing experimental community somewhere in the United States. A group of people visit it and explore all of the various aspects. Some of them joined up and stayed on and some are rebels and refuse to join and go away.

This raises a lot of problems about the design of cultural patterns and individual freedom under planning and it's stirred up a lot of discussion. Joseph Wood Krutch, in his book, *The Measure of Man*, spends two or three chapters tearing it down. *Life Magazine* attacked it as a vicious travesty on a good life, but I still believe in it. I still think that we have got to face up to facts about planning and using intelligence rather than accident to arrive at successful cultural patterns.[42]

- — (1969), Chapter 4, "The Experimental Analysis of Behavior", pp. 86–87, mentions gestalt psychology.
- — (1974), Chapter 5, "Perceiving", pp. 76–77, contains a brief comment related to gestalt psychologists.

41 OK, Fred. Sorry we asked. Wheeler was interested in the work of Guthrie. See Wheeler Interview, p. 77.

42 Needless to say, the interviewers acquired and read the already nine-year old *Walden Two* quickly after the interview. The writers were not alone in not having read it at the time. It attracted little notice when first written but sales continued to grow as the book became a cult item. Skinner describes the history of its phenomenal growth, Skinner (1983), pp. 251–252, 311–312, 341–342. Many others came to believe in it and a number of actual Walden communities were organised. Skinner visited at least one of them himself. Objections to the idea of a planned community "conditioned to moderation" centred on the concept of the some or many conditioning others in a determined plan of value positions. Skinner reported to the interviewers in a later discussion that "committees", set up to determine policy for the community, were always begging for members. Rather than everyone wishing to partici-

R.W.H. Does the whole idea of conditioning hold any fear for you?

---

pate in the "planning", individuals avoided the opportunity. It would seem that often, evolving behavioral interaction rather than planned consensus won the day and that "accident", rather than planning, remained the modal method of existence.

Of course, if planning did continue with individuals or one individual willing to do the planning, the worst scenario pertains; that is, the masses are conditioned according to the determination of the few (or one). In other words, things tend to regress to the *status quo*. In a society which has agreed to accept the idea of living a life subject to deliberate planned conditioning there is implied thoughtful prior agreement presumably determined through intelligent action. In the status quo, conditioning is not subject to any intelligence.

- B.F. Skinner (1948), *Walden Two*, first published in 1948 and later issued in 1969 with a new preface, could well serve as a handbook on the design of cultural patterns. The dialogues among the chief characters in the novel provide expository essays on Skinner's translation of the findings of the science of behaviour to the design of culture as well as a forum for the repudiation of the standard criticism of the work. Of special interest to educators are the segments of the novel dealing with the nurturing of infants, Chapter 12, pp. 95–99, and the education of children, Chapter 13 and 14, pp. 100–115. Commentary on approaches to teaching are included in Chapter 15. References in the novel to the major themes in this interview are cited at the appropriate places in the interview notes. Among the fourteen Skinner texts used as primary sources for notes, five are critical to an understanding of Skinner's position on "behavioral engineering" and the design of cultural patterns, *Walden Two* (1948), *Contingencies of Reinforcement* (1969), *Beyond Freedom and Dignity* (1978), *Reflections on Behaviorism and Society* (1978), and *Upon Further Reflections* (1987). The 1978 and 1987 publications focus primarily on "the commitment to an experimental analysis of behavior and its uses in the interpretation of human affairs." Skinner (1987), p. vii.

- — (1969), Section III, pp. 1–79, discusses contingencies of reinforcement and the design of cultures. Chapter 2, Utopia As An Experimental Culture, and Chapter 3, "The Environmental Solution, addresses and expands the discussion in the interview of the centrality of the scientific study of human behavior in the design of culture.

- — (1971), *Beyond Freedom and Dignity* extended many of the ideas introduced in *Walden Two*. Unlike *Walden Two*, the book is a non-fictionalized exposition of Skinner's position which calls for the development and utilization of a technology of behavior in the design of culture. Particularly related

B.F.S.   Any kind of power that man can get hold of strikes fear in my heart. I am just as afraid of the science of behavior as I am of the science of atomic physics, not because they both couldn't be used for the improvement of man's condition, but because they might fall into the hands of the wrong people and be used for just the opposite purpose. That's one of the reasons I go around shouting about the dangers of behavioral control because they could be badly misused unless people are aware of it.

The solution is not to deny that people can be controlled[43], which is what other people try to do, or to suppose we must cut it all out and stop being scientists, that this is somehow rather horrible. That's silly. What we have to do is make use of this knowledge for the ultimate goals of human existence.[44]

---

   to this segment of the interview is Chapter 8, "The Design of a Culture", pp. 161–163, which treats diversity within a planned setting.

- — (1974), Chapter 12, "The Question of Control", pp. 202–206, addresses the "evolution of a culture".

- — (1978), Chapter 5, "*Walden Two* Revisited", pp. 56–66. Skinner described circumstances, events and influences which stimulated his writing Walden II. He addresses problems of society within the context of the science of human behavior. Chapter 16, "*Walden* (One) and *Walden Two*", pp. 188–194. Skinner discusses the content of the two *Waldens* and comments of the 1948 Life magazine criticism of the novel. Chapter 1, "Human Behavior and Democracy", pp. 13–15, discusses cultural control. Chapter 2, "Are We free to Have a Future?", pp. 28–31, discusses the design of the future.

- — (1987), Chapter 3, "News from Nowhere, 1984", pp. 33–50, is a report by Burris, a resident of *Walden Two*, who through an extended conversation with Arthur Blair, a visitor to the community, updates life at Walden Two. The conversation of the two characters extends and updates the rationale for the structure and mode of operation of *Walden Two*.

43 In personal conversation with the interviewers, Skinner described life under authority epochs discussed earlier in the preface (p. 12).

44 "Anyone who denies the possibilities of behavior control is a fool", Skinner told the interviewers in later conversation at his home.

- B.F. Skinner (1948), Chapter 29, pp. 251–276 and Chapter 33, pp. 294–300, are particularly relevant. The discussions of the principles in this chapter treat such issues as the planned society, the tyranny of planning, behavioral control, political control and freedom. Some of these issues appear in a more fully developed form in *Beyond Freedom and Dignity* (1971). Some interesting material relating to ethical training through a controlled social environment appears in Chapter 14, pp. 104–115.

R.W.H. Yes, you are certainly aware of the implication of what you are doing.

B.F.S. Well, it certainly has ramifications in every walk of life. The reason I am interested in applying this first in education is that people can't really complain very much about your being a despot or a tyrant in a school room because, after all, you don't get much out of it personally and you don't teach so you can go out and stop somebody on the street and ask him a question and he gives you the answer. They are not trying to gain control over people in that sense. You use your control for their benefit[45]. So I feel reasonably comfortable in applying this in education.

• — (1953), Chapter 11, "A Science of Behavior", pp. 11–22, chapter XXVIII, "Designing a Culture", pp. 426–436, and chapter XXIX, "The Problem of Control", pp. 437–449, reflect Skinner's concerns about making use of knowledge.

• — (1959), Part I, "The Implications of a Science of Behavior for Human Affairs, Especially for the Concept of Freedom" contains three chapters, "Freedom and the Control of Men", "The Control of Human Behavior" (abstract), and "Some Issues Concerning the Control of Human Behavior". All three papers were written after the publication of *Walden Two*, and develop and expand some of the ideas introduced in that text. Skinner addresses Joseph Wood Krutch's criticism of *Walden Two*. "Some Issues Concerning the Control of Human Behavior" represents Skinner's side of a 1956 debate with Carl R. Rogers at a meeting of the American Psychological Association.

• — (1969), Chapter 1, "The Role of the Environment", pp. 42–45, deals specifically with the fear of control as well as objections to a designed culture.

• — (1971), Chapter 2, "Freedom" pp. 39–43, discusses freedom from control. Chapter 8, "The Design of a Culture", pp. 171–175, and "Countercontrol", pp. 180–183 addresses the issue of control raised in this interview.

• — (1974), Chapter 7, "Thinking", pp. 112–113, Chapter 12, "The Question of Control", pp. 189–206, deals with ethics, counter control, compassion, freedom and the evolution of culture. Chapter 14, "Summing Up", pp. 242–244, describes democracy as a version of counter control.

45 This is the crux of the problem. One person's heaven is another person's hell. Would one wish to live in B.F. Skinner's Utopia? As he suggests, one can feel" free, even though, intellectually, one could accept Skinner's point that we are all products of a chaotic conditioned experience, some "feel" free in their current state. If "God" wished us to be without "sin" he would have made us so and we wouldn't have known the difference. "God" in "His wisdom" chose not to do so. Skinner would want us "without sin" and, if the contingencies of reinforcement were correct, we wouldn't know the difference

If I were applying it in industry, for example, to control workers or if I were applying it in government, I would have battles on my hands that I can avoid by working in education.[46]

R.W.H.   Well, I guess that's right. Is everyone conditioned? I assume that they are from everything else that you have said. Can a person fight conditioning? I suppose that you would deny any type of moral sense or another kind of sense that would prevent a person from being conditioned?[47]

B.F.S.   You can't prevent a person from being conditioned, however, he may exist under circumstances where other variables are working which will off-set the effect of conditioning. It will be very poor engineering if you didn't make sure that something else wasn't opposing the thing you want to produce here. Brainwashing is presumably a kind of conditioning which makes the individual immune to revolt. It makes the actual conditioner immune to revolt. You not only condition someone, but you make perfectly sure that he will never try to oppose this.[48] In other cases you always have to face the facts that when you bring about this change that

---

either. Some would not choose to live in Skinner's world without sin anymore than Mark Twain wanted to go to Heaven, a place with no swearing, no drink, no poker – only heavenly choirs and angels. Twain (1962), pp. 8–13.

46 And yet, education is allegedly that means by which a society attempts to transmit to an ensuing generation that which it values. If behavioral science were to succeed when applied in education, the one (or many) in control would hold power, indeed. For a more extended commentary, see Houghton (1965).

• B.F. Skinner (1978), Chapter 1, "Human Behavior and Democracy", pp. 8–13, discusses social control and counter control within the context of government. Chapter 17, "Freedom and Dignity Revisited", pp. 195–198, again considers freedom and control.

47 This seems a particularly naïve question but it was asked before *Beyond Freedom and Dignity*. The interviewers are now sensitive to the Skinnerian idea of the continuous interactive process of differentiated and undifferentiated shaping of behavior occurring in life process.

48 In a pure behavioral control sense, the program would assure that the subject would never know that it had happened to him/her, anymore than or any less that a totally self conscious individual would recognise that he/she was the product of a lifelong conditioning process which has produced an organism to a greater or lesser degree unconscious of the fact that it had happened.

the individual knows you are doing it and that knowledge itself is something itself which may bring about an opposite change.

If you try to use a student in an experiment, he may deliberately do the opposite of what he is inclined to do just to wreck the experiment. This is not unlawful behavior.[49]

- B.F. Skinner (1987), Chapter 1, "Why We Are Not Acting to Save the World", pp. 1–14, addresses the separation of behavior and consequences as central to contemporary national and global problems. The overall problem of cultural design provides the context for the discussion. Chapter 2, "What is Wrong with Daily Life in the Western World", pp. 15–31, identifies "the erosion of the strengthening effect of reinforcement" as critical to an understanding of the contemporary problems of Western cultures.

49 The interviewers, with hindsight, recognise that the behavioral modification strategies of radical behaviorism do not operate like medieval torture chambers. Reinforcement occurs after indeliberate voluntary behaviors in the subject which represent operants in the direction of desired behavioral change. "Right" behaviors are reinforced. "Wrong" behaviors are not punished with blows from long black whips. They are "extinguished" subtly with withholding of reinforcement.

There is, of course, negative reinforcement, that is, reinforcement occurs as punishment ceases and the client "feels so good" to be free of the aversive control. Behaviors tend to be prevented through aversion. Behaviors tend to be changed positively through reinforcement. Skinner is also speaking of the need to develop positive contingency fields which are naturally encouraging to desired behavioral change.

The interview ends abruptly as the tape runs out.

R.H. Wheeler courtesy Babson College Alumni Bulletin, Babsonia, *Babson Park, Massachu-setts vol. xxix Nov. 1961, No. 1.*

R.W.H.   We are sitting in the living room of Dr R.H. Wheeler in Wellesley, Massachusetts. We have come to Wellesley to talk with Dr Wheeler about organismic psychology and learning.

Professor Wheeler, in the beginning can we discuss what you assume to be, the nature of man. Is man merely what you might call the upper end of the biological continuum?

R.H.W.   Why, yes indeed, Ray. Man is, at the what I call, the upper end of a biological continuum. Certainly, but in my opinion since this is a discussion of the organismic point of view there is nothing basically different in principle between the different levels of the animal kingdom in as far as the basic laws of their constitution are concerned.

For example, all organisms, in my thinking at least, from the simplest to the complex, obey or follow these organismic laws which I am sure some of which you have in mind. For example, the whole is more than the sum of the parts whether you are an amoeba or a human being.[1] And as

---

1   Wheeler gets right to the point. He begins with wholes and suggests that the whole is more than the sums that go to make it. Wheeler is wrong in that he credits the interviewers with recognition of the primacy of the organismic laws in his thinking.

• Wheeler, R.H., (1929) *The Science of Psychology* . Chapter V, "Intelligent Behavior: Direct Methods", pp. 117–130, discusses intelligent behavior from studies of crawfish and chimpanzees. In pages 130–149, also in Chapter V, Wheeler describes degrees of complexity in the exploration of intelligence among organisms of varying complexity. "Preface", pp. viii–ix and "Introduction", pp. 16–18, provide introductory material relating to the basic principle of Wheeler's thinking – "The whole is more than the sum of its parts."

• — (1930) *Readings in Psychology*. Reading I, "The Individual and the Group. An Application of Eight Organismic Laws", pp. 7–10, discusses the first organismic law – "The whole is more than the sum of its parts", in the context of the social group, the individual and the physical world; pp. 8 and 9 of Reading I contain a brief commentary on the source of human nature.

you come up the animal scale the greater complexity that you meet as you come up the scale and involves the emergence of new properties, new phenomena that you did not have before in lower levels. That is the main difference. The laws are not different. The phenomena are different.

R.W.H. I have noticed that in your writing that you say the behavior of man is similar but more highly developed than that of lower animals. That is exactly the same kind of thing, of course, that the behaviorist would say in the beginning.[2] You would say that, then, the differences between your organismic point of view and the behavioristic point of view is with respect to the complexities behind the behaviors of man.

R.H.W. Yes, primarily I should say the behaviorist, in my opinion, leaves out a lot of the important phenomena that, psychologically speaking, seems to be necessary to consider. That would become a little clearer, Ray, if you go specifically into some of the assumptions of the two schools.

---

2   The interviewer was dead wrong in assuming that Wheeler and the behaviorist are saying the same thing. They agree that humans are at the upper end of a biological continuum but Wheeler leaps to the assumption about the primacy of his organismic laws. The interviewer was bluffing.

• — (1923) "Introspection and Behavior", *Psychological Review*, Vol. XXV, pp. 103–115, presents a criticism of behaviorism focusing on its methodology.

• — (1931) "Errors in Recent Critiques of Gestalt Psychology I. Sources of Confusion" with F. Theodore Perkins and S. Howard Bartley, *Psychological Review*, Vol. 38, pp. 109–135. is one of a series of five articles dealing with gestalt. The reference cited above discusses misconceptions of the gestalt position and the source of the misconceptions. A rationale for the gestalt position is presented.

• — (1933) "Errors in the Critiques of Gestalt Psychology III. Inconsistencies in Thorndike's System", *Psychological Review*, with F. Theodore Perkins, Vol. 40, No. 4, July 1933, pp. 303–323, presents a discussion of the major assumption upon which Thorndike's system is based, as well as discussion of points relating to gestalt psychology which the authors believe Thorndike misconstrued.

• — (1935) "Organismic vs. Mechanistic Logic", *Psychological Review*, Vol. XLII, pp. 335–353, is a unique exploration of the "mechanistic-vitalistic" cycles in world society from a historical point of view. The article, not surprisingly, emerges as an attack on the "behavioristic-mechanistic" psychologies.

R.W.H. Right. We have noted when considering the idea of individual differences, for example, you say that newly born human organisms possess some established predispositions with which to face life. What do you mean by predispositions?

R.H.W. Well, Ray, let's put it this way. If you were a bond psychologist or a behaviorist,[3] either one, you would probably, now I may be wrong, but you would probably make the assumption something on the order of what John Locke made in his philosophy, that when you are born you don't know anything, there is nothing in your mind if you have one.[4] It's blank and experience comes in, grows, develops piecemeal, item by item, bit by bit, through the senses or through conditioning. Either way.

Now, according to the organismic psychologist, the position that I like, such a theory of the origin of mind is logically and factually wrong for this reason you are going to begin with separate sense impressions or separate responses that have to be bonded together by repetition, conditioning and what not. There is in my opinion nothing in forming a bond or a connection or in the conditioning process that generates anything. It can't, for instance, generate thinking or intelligence or anything of that sort by trying to put parts together. Without an emergent phenomenon you haven't got a whole.[5]

---

3 He is drawing the critical distinction between reflex arc psychology of Thorndike and Skinner's operant behaviorism.

4 Notice the qualifier here. He does not hesitate to begin to use the word, "mind", but senses a vulnerability and begs the question, casually, with "If you have one". He introduces the parts to wholes position immediately, finding his entry point in eighteenth century sense empiricism (Locke), which he immediately equates with nineteenth century behaviorism (Watson).

• Wheeler R.H. (1931) *The Laws of Human Nature*, Chapter I, "The Background of Contemporary Psychology", provides an overview of the development of the field of psychology through a discussion of conflicting points of view: pp. 24–31 deal with association psychology, behaviorism and attention psychology. Chapter II, "The Transition to Scientific Psychology", pp. 41–42, discusses behaviorism as an example of "atomism in modern psychology".

5 Skinner would say not that you have an emergent phenomenon, but that you have a new behavior, a new way of behaving. Wheeler prefers the almost mystical 'emergent' as adjective. Skinner favours the more simple expression of new behavior.

• Wheeler and Perkins, (1932) *The Science of Psychology*, Chapter II, "The Laws of Human Nature", pp. 16–37, describes the "fallacy of the mechanistic

Now the example, the classic example of that, comes from chemistry where you put hydrogen and oxygen together, you get water. Now water is composed of an entirely different set of properties from either hydrogen or oxygen so I don't see how of course we are boiling down a lot of stuff to a few words maybe too briefly, you can combine two sense impressions like the sound and visual sense impressions or two *muscular* responses or whatever you might want. I don't see how you can get those together, combine them, and get anything out of them without an emergence and that emergence is not predictable from what you put together.[6]

And so, that switches us to the other school if we want the answer. And now this is just my opinion. And that is this, that they are not born empty minded. The infant is born with a very feeble low level kind of an intelligence or, better say, a capacity to understand, a capacity to formulate meaning in his own mind[7] in the presence of stimulation, the challenge of stimulation. Now that doesn't have to be rehearsed, it doesn't have to be repeated. The response is effective under the right conditions the first time it occurs. The meaning is there. The understanding is there. It doesn't have to build up by a conditioning process. In fact, in my opinion, anything on the order of conditioning, of trial and error, results in anything only because the conditions under which we get these things, get the trial and error, are artificial. If the conditions were correctly set up at the level of the learner's understanding at the moment there would never be any-

---

point of view" and sets out the organismic view of human nature. Actually, modern neuroscientific theory seems more the old Thorndike bond psychology in that repeated neurological sensation "reinforces" or perhaps sustains previously received data. See note 6, page 37.

6   This is to suggest on the part of Wheeler that properties of base elementary antecedents cannot be used to predict properties in the combined elements without the introduction of "organismic" laws already obtaining. Skinner, on the other hand, does not seek nor need "phantom" laws to induce new behavior from old behavior, using logically successive intermediate micro behavioral changes predicted strategically and routed in single case access according to no universal "organismic" laws nor any other kind of universal necessity.

•   Wheeler, R.H. (1929), Introduction, pp. 16–17, provides a more detailed discussion of Wheeler's example of the relationship of water, hydrogen and oxygen to illustrate the concept of the "the whole is more than the sum of its parts".

7   Again, no hesitancy on using "mind".

thing such as trial and error. There would never be anything such as conditioning.[8]

So to me conditioning and trial and error or anything along that order are consequences of a misfit, a lack or a discrepancy between the situation impressed on the learner and the learner's capacity at that moment, and his level of maturation at that moment.[9]

---

8   Wheeler is describing what he assumes to be a predisposition in the infant to respond "mindfully" to stimuli. When Wheeler claims the "meaning is there", "the understanding is there", he would be saying that the infant has the capacity to respond to stimuli in terms of the reinforcing qualities generative in the interactive stimulus response sequencing. It is not unlike radar. Radar bounces sound signals off solids. Could this be called trial and error? Rather, it is "mindful" deliberate use of an external feedback mechanism seeking an appropriate response. If a solid feedback response is generated as new stimuli, an internal response mechanism allows specific decisions to be made. "Radar" is, in McLuhan's terminology, a tool, a medium, a sensory extension of man, McLuhan (1964), *Understanding Media*, Part I, pp. 3–30. The stimulus probes are not merely trial and error. They are determined purposeful gropings. For both Skinner and Wheeler, stimulus response interactions are purposeful. Wheeler sees such gropings as lawful. Skinner sees them as merely purposeful.

•   Wheeler (1931), Chapter IV, "The Development of Behavior", p. 119, presents a brief discussion of "growth potential" denying "trial and error". Chapter V, "The Laws of Learning" pp. 147–148, denies the function of trial and error in the context of animal behavior.

•   — (1932), Chapter XIX, "Theoretical Problems of Learning", pp. 356–357, treats the inadequacy of the concept of trial and error.

•   — (1940), Chapter VII, "Learning: General Problems", pp. 232–233, describes the source of the concept of trial and error.

9   In other words, learning is problem solving. If the stimulus environment generates problems (the need for new learning) the organism cannot initially comprehend it. It is faced with stimulus "overload" and the "warning" lights flash. Frantic response stimuli are generated in a panic condition, radar-like emergency operation. Normally equilibrium obtains only after recognisable external stimulus identification is established and a mindful low level intelligence condition is restored. In speaking of maturation, Wheeler is assuming that the interviewers understand his concept of pace or readiness to interact intelligently with a new problem stimulus.

•   Coghill (1929), *Anatomy and the Problem of Behavior*, pp. 85–86 discusses problem solving in Amblystoma.

R.W.H.   Yes. This gets into your whole conception of pace.[10]

R.H.W.   That's right. Definitely. Did I ever write about this famous pro, golf pro.[11] I don't believe I ever did, who tried these principles intuitively

---

10 By pace, Wheeler seems to mean maturational developmental sequencing. Such sequencing is highly individual as differentiated from the universal notions of classic developmentalists. Pace is in the continuous and interrelated growth/learning sequence. It would seem to relate to the organism's readiness to take on new learning and the process of integrating such learning. Pace then involves readiness, new exposure, an opportunity for new learning to settle, new maturity, new readiness as a cycle of pacing continues. A mechanical analogy might be that of a modern anti-locking braking mechanism on a motor car whereby as one braking wheel skids, it is automatically released and another wheel brakes until the first wheel is ready to become effective again as it senses a non-slippery surface.
   • Wheeler (1932), Chapter X, "The Measurement of Intelligence", p. 197, defines pacing. Chapter XVIII, "Control of the Learning Process – IV", p. 345, contains brief notes discussing pacing" as a learning problem. Chapter XXII, "Motivation", pp. 415–416, comments briefly on pacing within the context of the problem of motivation.
   • — (1940), Chapter VIII, "Learning: General Problems", pp. 230–232, discusses pacing and Chapter IX, "Learning: The More Precise Facts and Methods", pp. 256–258, discusses pacing as a learning problem.
   • — (1929), Chapter IV, "Intelligent Behavior: Indirect Methods", pp. 114–115, discusses the concept of pacing. Chapter XI, "Learning Behavior: The More Precise Facts and Methods", pp. 316–317, is a commentary on the inadequacy of trial and error learning within a fairly technical chapter on selected physiological aspects of learning.
11 The writers did not identify this specific illustration in Wheeler's writing. His publications are, however, sprinkled with a number of examples relating to the development of a proper golf swing to illustrate some of the organismic laws of learning. Wheeler (1922), p. 310, describes necessity for a moment of delay in the golf swing. Wheeler (1931), pp. 174–176, stresses the need for movement of the body as a whole during the swing and the material on pages 154–156 discuss the issue of practice and the problem of reversion and regression as they relate to golf. Wheeler (1931), p. 265, discusses the concept of initial delay to motor skills in the golf swing. Pages 267–269 include a discussion which seems the most closely related to the content in the interview. This citation treats pattern movement in golf and the law of field geneses applied to golf skills. Did he play golf himself? His biographical sheet says so. (Biographical summary written by Helen Tatum, 1927.)

when teaching golf without knowing what the psychological basis of it was. Nobody learning golf under this particular pro, I can't even give you a name, that was years ago in Iowa. Anybody learning golf under this pro executed successfully, every step of the way, what was asked of him without making any mistakes unless it was by accident.[12]

There was no trial and error in learning golf. There was no dubbing, no cutting, no slicing, no topping, no mistakes made. Every performance was successful the first time it was tried. Things could go wrong, he might be sick today, he might be distracted, or some accident, but the principle seemed to hold definitely throughout and this is how he did it.

Instead of puting the driver in the player's hand and starting off with a tee shot or some complicated shot in which he would have to master direction and force and distance at the same time, he started right at the cup of the green one inch from the cup. Now your goal, you see organismic behavior by definition, is all goal directed. There isn't any such thing as performance that isn't goal directed. The goal is to drop the ball in the cup one inch away. He tells you how to hold the club and your stance and so on and you can be successful. Next time, you don't repeat anything. There is no drill in the old fashioned sense of the term. It's practice, but not drill.[13] Then he moves the ball two inches away, another inch away, then three, then four, then back gradually. When it is back far enough, you say the object is to get as near to the cup as you can within a large circle and he marks a circle with chalk or something. Then he gradually reduces the circle. The goal is always reached and there is no trial and error.[14]

---

12 He means here interruption of the growth process through breakdown of concentration, a slight (or major) misbehavior or some such contingency.

13 Wheeler considers "practice" as mindful, thoughtful, understanding action, a total maturational process. He would think of drill as related to "muscle memory" or neural conditioning of the bond psychologists. Rather, the process bears a cognitive element which preconsciously allows the new behavior to find relationship with known past behaviors. It seems strangely like appercaption.

14 One might ask, where was that pro when one needed him? Strange that the writers have never heard of any of his pupils on the PGA tour. The story may be apocryphal, but the point is taken. What Wheeler describes here as goal centred behavior is strikingly similar to Skinner's operant conditioning. While Skinner might not begin at the hole, he would, as has Wheeler, divide the ultimate task into operants, small steps, always successfully attained, reinforced immediately and positively by success, though with a redefinition of

That's what I mean when an animal is confronted with a problem and has to adjust through trial and error. It just means that the problem is too

---

success, more like reduced margins of "error". Again, there is no trial and error. Each effort is purposeful.

The distinction is that Wheeler's learner would have the whole task in view, it would be goal centered, inevitable, driven by the organismic laws, the behavior would represent new maturity. It is not to say that there might be occasions of imprecision caused by carelessness, loss of concentration, external distraction, but the "learning" would have been accomplished.

Contrastingly, in Skinner's operant learning, the learner may or may not have had the "end in mind", may not see the task as a whole. Each operant would be a part toward a whole. With Wheeler, each "operant" would be a whole. Interestingly, at the point of mastery, Skinner's behavior would have become a whole whereas at the point of mastery, Wheeler's behavior would be a conceptualized whole, a process whole, attaining real wholeness only when accomplished in perfect accordance with the organismic laws (law of least effort, for example). To readers familiar with behavioral principles it is obvious that Wheeler makes no distinction between Thorndyke's associationist principles, Watson's stimulus response behaviorism with the notion of the reflex arc and Skinner's operant conditioning.

The failure of general readers to recognize or acknowledge these differences is the cause of much of the antagonism to Skinner's psychological and social thinking. It is remindful of Bishop Berkeley's "immaterialism" being misunderstood by Dr Johnson when he tripped on a stone and hurt his foot. Johnson's toe perceived the material quality of the stone, illustrating the key to Berkeley's position, "To be is to be perceived". Johnson had probably only heard rumours. He didn't read it. Many have failed to really read Skinner.

- Wheeler R.H. (1930), Reading VIII, "The Solving of Problem–Situations by Pre-School Children: An Analysis", pp. 114–115, points out the "wastefulness" of trial and error as well as the mistake of conventionally conceived drill and practice. It also introduces the idea of pacing.
- — (1931), Chapter VI, "The Laws of Learning", pp. 174–176, utilizes the example of learning to play golf to illustrate organismic laws of learning II through V. Laws VI through VII, on pp. 176–177, illuminate the discussion of learning to play golf contained in the interview. Wheeler's concern for the proper formulation of problems, observation, and logical thinking permeate this volume. A discussion relating to these concerns may be found in Chapter II, "The Transition to Scientific Psychology", pp. 33–40, as well as in Chapter VI, "The Laws of Learning", p. 150.
- — (1929), *The Science of Psychology*, p. 310, extends the golf metaphor re: the concept of "initial delay" in the learning process.

difficult for him and never should have been given him.[15] If you have the learning process correctly or properly under control, there is never any trial and error.[16] I don't think there is any trial and error in animal behavior where they confront situations that are natural to them. Mothers teach their young. Whenever any learner confronts a problem that is beyond his level of maturation[17] at the time, he will display trial and error, but he is fishing for more understanding. That's what he is doing. It isn't mechanical conditioning.[18]

R.W.H. Most interesting. This reminds me of Guthrie.[19] Guthrie said that one exposure results in learning as opposed to what some of the other behaviorists said.

R.H.W. Yes, I know that Guthrie was quite friendly to some of these ideas, I've got his book upstairs. In fact we used to correspond. There is another little thing in that connection I would like to mention because I don't know why, but there are so many psychologists now here I am sort of condemning my own profession, but there are many psychologists, and other scientists as well who think that most of science is observing. It's only half of science that is observing.[20] There is just as much thinking necessary and correct comprehension of a problem in the first place as

---

15 One more organism on stimulus overload.
16 Nor is there with Skinner's operant conditioning. There is merely control of contingencies.
17 Maturation and/or growth is critical to Wheeler. The organism must be ready. This developmental character to Wheeler's thinking is critical to the understanding of him.
18 The notion of "fishing for understanding" is like the previously cited radar metaphor. There is at least low level intelligence behind the action. The action is probing for meaning, a recognizable stimulus signal to which there can be a recognized response. Wheeler is right when he says it is not "mechanical" conditioning, but it surely might be a kind of conditioning. For Skinner, learning is change in behavior with no intervening variables. For Wheeler, learning is insight. If insight has obtained, proper behaviour remains potential, if imminent. The problem with this writer's own golf game is that he has learned the game according to Wheeler's learning theory and perfection remains imminent, but mostly unobtainable.
19 Hilgard (1956), *Theories of Learning.* Chapter 3, "Guthrie's Contiguous Conditioning", pp. 48–81.
20 While not directed at Skinner, Wheeler is guilty of painting with a broad

there is in observing. You have to have logic and most psychologists are not properly impressed with logic[21] and for that reason they waste an awful lot of time in trying to solve problems which are no good in the first place. The conception of problem is faulty.

I will give you an example. Now I have insisted for years that you can't understand human or animal behavior without the law of parsimony. Physicists call it the law of least action[22] on account of certain technical require-

---

brush. Skinner specifically calls attention to the necessity for thought and conceptualizing. (See Skinner Interview pages 59–60.)

21 In his enthusiasm for logic, one would suspect that Wheeler had read C.S. Pierce. It would be strange if he had not although much of his work was not readily available until after 1931. We have found no direct connection between Pierce, William James or John Dewey and Wheeler. Interestingly, John Dewey studied with Pierce and G. Stanley Hall at Johns Hopkins. Wheeler could well have been taught by Pierce at Clark University. G, Stanley Hall did teach Wheeler at Clark and, as President of Clark, denied Pierce a position there in 1913. Wheeler, it is remembered, graduated in 1912 and took his advanced degree in 1915.

22 In physics the concept of a law of least action has origins described in the work of Philip E.F. Jourdain (1913) who dates it to Pierre Louis Moreau Maupertius, 1698–1759. It is central to the work of the 20th century physicist/mathematician, Richard Feynman. It was a key idea in his dissertation, *The Principle of Least Action in Quantum Mechanics*, for his doctoral degree awarded at Princeton in 1942. He returned to it throughout his career of problem solving. Gleick (1992).

It seems likely that Wheeler adopted this phrase to his personal usage. As to whether his use of it defines a "law" is the question. Is he saying that always, in the process of problem solving, a sub-intelligent or low-intelligent or an unconscious intelligent potential in organisms leaves the organism poised to respond to the most immediate stimulus cue? Does this eliminate random trial and error entirely, or does it mean only that when the organism attains a viable attention state, an emergence from a state of super stimulation, does the "law" of least action, parsimony, begin to pertain? In the interviewers consideration of this question, it's plausibility is confirmed when one imagines high activity states running down, or calming to a natural stasis, as energy is played out. There is always the drive to stasis – from the complex exhausting state of super stimulated frantic action to the calming state of inaction. Organisms can only survive in a condition of limited purposeful action. Even in a process of conditioning there could be imagined a low level intelligence, unconscious, perhaps, that gives direction to responses. Perhaps this low level unconscious determination of behavioral response is stimulated

ments, but it is a law of economy. A law of parsimony.[23] Well, now actually it isn't well enough understood but as I see it, you couldn't make any prediction whatever at any time without the law. It is the only law of prediction there is.[24] Because it is the only basic principle that actually accounts for, or has to do with, order, orderliness, predictability. I wonder how many psychologists know that it is this law that is the basis of accu-

---

by this very basic "law" of parsimony, a drive towards least action solution of the immediate stimulus engendered "problem".

* Jourdain (1913) *The Principle of Least Action.*

23 The interviewers have not been able to identify the use of this word among physicists. However, a number of mathematicians consulted have indicated that it may well have a usefulness in the description of the process of exclusion of assumptions as described by Wheeler. It seems likely that he adopted the word to his personal usage. As to whether it defines a "law" is questionable.

* Wheeler (1929), Chapter III, "Social Behavior and Its Conditions", pp. 79–83, presents commentary on the law of least action within the context of a social setting, negating the concept of trial and error. Chapter III, "Biological Organization", pp. 82–88, develops the concept of the "law of least action" within both a physical and biological context.

* — (1931), Chapter V, "The Laws of Perception", pp. 134–135, comments on the law of least action relative to perception. Chapter VI, "The Laws of Learning", p. 176, includes the law of least action in a summary of the laws of learning, pp. 173–177. Chapter VIII, "The Laws of Personality", pp. 218–220, provides a discussion of the law of least action as it functions within the context of personality.

* — (1932), Chapter II, "The Laws of Human Nature", pp. 26–31, develops an understanding of the law of least action applying the law to human beings and to social behavior.

24 In other words, the one thing that can be counted on is that, all things being equal, organisms will proceed (behave) with prospect of least action, the least effort, parsimoniously.

It would seem that if the law of parsimony is in effect in the solving of the "separate little problems", then the successive solutions of them, as the organism seeks a "conception of the whole", cannot be called "trial and error", but are, rather, stimulus probes driven by the law, as a low order of intelligence toward the solution of the larger problem. Wheeler does not explain the ground of the law. Is it, as the interviewers suggest, in a genetic base intelligence or is it learned, perhaps pre-natally, or post-natally, or is it merely organic, that is, in nature itself, and perhaps not exclusively a phenomenon of life?

racy in mathematical reasoning.[25] It is when a mathematician starts with
the fewest possible number of assumptions. If he starts with one too many
he is going to end wrong and if he takes one step too many in thinking
through the problem from an axiom or proposition to the solution, if he
puts in one extra step too many, he gets the wrong answer. The procedure
must be absolutely minimal. It is the shortest distance so to speak, logical
distance, between comprehensions of the problem and the solution. No
extra assumptions, no extra steps.

Now, I don't care what the situation is, nothing can be solved, no
movement can be explained or predicted without this law. Then, why
don't psychologists use it? The only reason why there is any learning at all
is the existence of this law. Let me show you how.

Take a rat in a checkerboard maze where it is all divided into little
compartments and doorways from each compartment emptying into adja-
cent compartments. He is hungry, you put him in the starting box. He
doesn't know a thing about the pattern of the maze. He can't see at all. He
isn't oriented to the patterns of the maze. He knows nothing about it. All
he knows, all he can see, and all he can understand at that moment is that
one little compartment and how to get through it. Well he has to get
through it all, he has to be under the laws of nature of the entire universe
as far as that's governed. He has to apply that law to get through the
compartment. He can't do it without it.

Now, in getting through he is going to take the shortest path through
that compartment as it appears to him at that moment. If his head is facing
one door he will go through that one. If his head is facing through that
door he will go through that one. He will take the shortest path. Then he
comes to the next compartment. He has to solve that problem separately[26]
out of relation to the first one because they don't form a pattern so he
reapplies the law and he goes through that one even though it may be at an
angle from the first one. Now he does that for each of the separate compartments. That's why his performance is trial and error because he can't
see the whole thing, it is beyond his comprehension and he does solve,
without any trial and error,[27] separate little problems he confronts in succession by the simplest means that he can.

---

25 The principle of "least action" again. See note 23.
26 This illustrates Wheeler's idea of the solution of small problems driven by the
    organismic laws toward the solution of the large problem (insight).
27 This is reminiscent of an infant moving and stretching to find its voice in
    anticipation of crying. It is remindful also of a golfer's motion prior to swing-

R.W.H. What are the stimulus factors which effect the rat's decision with respect to the laws of parsimony?

R.H.W. Well, he will vacillate. He's nervous. *He is* in action, of course. He is in motion most of the time.[28] Usually if his head is facing one he will take that one. If he is distracted and he sees some motion and he turns the other way, he will take that one then. We don't always know those things in detail, but we do know logically he has got to, he can't help it. What happens to be the shortest path depends on the circumstances at that moment. We don't always know what they are. Even though we don't, we have to assume it, or you can't explain anything. The reason why I mention all of this is that as he finally succeeds in getting to the box, the food

---

ing a golf club (waggle) seeking to find the most efficient and effective swing path toward striking the ball. Golf instruction theory is a most sophisticated body of investigation into the diagnosis and prescription of a psychomotive activity and has become infinitely more so since Wheeler's time. See Ledbetter (1991).

- Wheeler (1932), Chapter VIII, "Analysis of the Learning Process: Maturation, Goal, Insight", pp. 253–259, discusses insight as part of the learning process with "practical consequences" for classrooms.

28 It is interesting to watch an organism learning the solution to a problem. At the moment of Wheeler's insight, which seems little more than Skinner's learning, higher rates of action are initiated. Skinner explains it as the result of the reinforcement of "getting it right". Action continues to accelerate as the organism races to complete the larger problem solving. Organisms in such a state are attention centred, self initiated. They are not in a behavior-neutral state. Observe individuals in queues behaving neutrally as they patiently wait their turn in line. Suddenly a new service point opens and there is a feverish rush to move to a favoured position at the head of a new queue.

If, then, rapid learning is to be equated with insight, then intelligence is related to the ability to learn parsimoniously in an *acceleration* of the learning process. Low level learning is tedious, like lighting a fire with damp kindling. Intelligence is determined less on genetic intelligence and more on accelerating learning, in any organism – irrespective of predisposition.

- Wheeler (1929), Chapter XVI, "The Nervous System in Its Relation to Behavior", p. 497, equates laws of behavior with laws of growth.
- — (1930), Reading VIII, "The Solving of Problem–Situations by Pre-School Children: An Analysis", pp. 114–115, indicates the "paramount importance for the educator of understanding fully the nature of insight in order that mental development may take place in the child with the least amount of wasted time and energy.

box, he has been through the maze once and a little emergence occurs, a little insight develops, a little maturation takes place and he has a vague idea of the pattern of the maze in relation of the food box to the starting box. It's very vague, very unstable to be put back in there, but there is enough of that orientation to the pattern as a whole so that he will not wander so far to one side or the other in a succession of little separate disconnected responses connected only by the desire to forage ahead to find something.

Now this is what I am building up to. When the orientation is completed he has now discovered. It isn't conditioning. It is discovering. It is growth. It is the development of understanding and insight. He's paced himself. Now he can see the thing whole and he takes the shortest path to get on to this re-oriented situation. He still takes the shortest path. Now, from the starting box to the food box he takes a path because it is the shortest, that's the reason why he takes it. That, by the way, is the criterion of an intelligent response being able to take the shortest route. Under other circumstances, it is the criterion of an insight. Seeing a thing whole enables you to do it.[29]

R.W.H.   Is intelligence equated with insight?

---

29 It seems to the interviewers that rather than intelligence being equated with insight, rapid learning is equated with insight. The metaphor here is that the physical phenomenon of burning (oxidation) is like learning. In that explosion is rapid burning, insight is rapid learning. To Wheeler, learning is problem solving and the route to learning is in the solution of small problems. Is this not very much the same as Skinner's route to *conditioned* learning wherein the Wheeler "small problems" are, in fact, Skinner's "operants"? With Wheeler, progression is drive to closure, to insight, to the solution of the total problem in learning. With Skinner progression is reinforcement driven as each appropriate behavior is reinforced in movement toward the ultimate correct behavior.

- Wheeler (1929), Chapter IX, "Learning Grosser Facts and Methods", pp. 261–264, discusses insight within the context of the laws of contiguity.
- — (1931), Chapter VI, "The Laws of Learning", pp. 162–163, equates learning with growth of insight. P. 17, see Law of Learning VIII.
- — (1940), Chapter VII, "Intelligent Behavior: Direct Methods", pp. 191–192, discusses the concept of "insight" and pp. 193–196 describe supporting experimental data.
- — (1932), Chapter V, "Evolution of the Learning Process", pp. 82–88, explores insight through goldfish and chick studies.

R.H.W. The same thing. As far as this session is concerned, regard them as the same thing.[30]

R.W.H. The same thing. All right then.

R.H.W. Intelligence grows. I don't believe in native endowment, you know.

R.W.H. All right. Well say it, go ahead.

R.H.W. Well, that's not what I had in mind next. The organismic theory of heredity is very different from the orthodox theory. I don't know how much you have gone into that or how much your students go into that, but you know that there is a very prominent and, in my mind, a very remarkable movement in biological thinking in the last fifty years which is all opposed to the gene theory in its original form.[31] All opposed to any such thing as a fixed heredity. That we are born with an IQ of just so much and no more, that it comes from the germ plasm and all that. I am very much opposed to all of that.

---

30 It would again seem to the writers that learning is to be equated with insight. Does it thus mean that intelligence = insight = learning? One is reminded that Skinner would also say that intelligence is related directly to behavior, that is, what the organism can do.
- Wheeler (1929), Chapter V, "Intelligent Behavior: Direct Methods", p. 126, includes brief commentary regarding criterion of insight.
- — (1932), Chapter I, "Point of View", pp. 2–4, introduces some basic organismic views of intelligence. Chapter IX, "The Source of Intelligent Behavior", pp. 162–172, discusses heredity and environment in relation to the problem of intelligence and the "so-called constancy of I!". The nature, limitation and relativity of inheritance is discussed in pages 157–161.
- — (1930), Reading I, "The Individual and the Group: An application of Eight Organismic Laws", pp. 10–12, presents a discussion within the context of the second organismic law – "Parts derive their properties from the whole: as the determinants of the development of intelligent behavior in humans."

31 Wheeler R.H. (1929), Chapter VI, "Emotive Behavior", pp. 174–175, contains a brief discussion which takes issue with the common view of gene transmitted inheritance. Chapter XVII, "The Nervous System in Its Relation to Behavior" cites the work of G.E. Coghill (1929) in relation to the nervous system raising doubt about the function of synapse. Coghill's theory of "maturation versus exercise" is discussed on pp. 495–496.

For example, it isn't heredity at all that determines that your head is where it is, or that you've got one head. That has nothing to do with it. Nothing whatever. I know a lot of physiologists, Child is one of them and Coghill[32] is another. There have been a lot of studies, but now in the hundreds, that demonstrate the limitations of the old gene theory of heredity and which you have everything laid out in advance in the germ plasm.

Now, another thing. Heredity doesn't determine where you put your bones. There are laws of engineering[33] as I call them. Laws of growth, laws of dynamics. The engineer uses these laws when he builds a skyscraper, or a boat or a bridge. He uses these laws. He has to. He couldn't build good structures. Nature, so to speak, is an engineer, figuratively speaking. The engineer got his laws from nature and these laws account for the outcome of much of growth. I am not denying heredity. There are three things that are necessary for the outcome of an organism. Destiny, if you want to call it that.

The three causal factors that cannot be separated from each other. One is heredity, but is far more limited than most geneticists, American geneticists, have been willing to admit. The second is these laws of growth, the laws of engineering. The third is environment. Just to illustrate what I call organismic laws. How does an organism know where to deposit a bone. How does he know where to grow his bones? There is nothing in his genes that tells him where to put a bone, nothing. Not one identical thing. A growing organism has to discover through some selective process where to

---

- — (1931). In Chapter IV, "The Development of Behavior", pp. 107–111, Wheeler discusses Coghill's study of the nervous system of the salamander embryo in *Anatomy and the Problem of Behavior*.
- — (1940), Chapter XIV, "The Nervous System in Relation to Behavior – 2", pp. 398–403, reports Coghill's experimental work in embryology and conclusions to be drawn from the work: pp. 406–408 report Coghill's theory of development and learning and pp. 408–410 report reactions criticising his work.
- Coghill (1929), Lecture III, "The Growth of the Nerve Cell and the Interpretation of Behavior", pp. 79–110, provides source material for Wheeler's discussion.
32 Coghill (1929), pp. 88–89.
- Child (1928), "The Beginnings of Unity and Order in Living Things," *The Unconscious A Symposium* provides supportive data for Wheeler's thinking.
33 Wheeler (1931), Chapter III, "Biological Organization", pp. 67–68, 76–77, 90–91, describe the laws of heredity as laws of dynamics.

put his bones. And how does it know, so to speak, how to put them? Stress lines develop. Just exactly the laws of engineering. With engineering they calculate in advance where stress lines develop in a bridge or a building. He has to put in supportive structures to take up those stresses when it gets the weight of the structure put together, so that even a single cell growing lays a membrane right down through the center when it gets heavy enough or big enough, massive enough. It will lay a membrane down through the center. Divide that membrane is a supporting structure [*sic*]. It may not divide, fall apart, the membrane is put down there, deposited there along the stress lines and that's been worked out. Text books in biology have worked all that out and diagrammed it so the stress line the embryo deposits, calcium along the stress lines that develop the bones. Then masses of tissue accumulate. That's how it knows where to put those bones! Heredity doesn't tell the organism where to put the bones, Ray, that is what I mean by the importance of logic. Logic should tell anybody that heredity couldn't do all this. It doesn't possess the mechanism by which it could do it. Now it can do a lot and does a lot but it can't do all that its assumed it can do.[34]

R.W.H. Would Darwin or Mendel go with your thinking?

R.H.W. No, Lamarck[35] would, definitely. The modern biologists who have developed these principles are mostly Lamarckians.[36] You see, the

34 Wheeler (1935), *Psychological Review*, "Organismic Logic vs. Mechanistic Logic", pp. 345–353.
• Child (1928), "The Beginnings of Unity and Order in Living Things", pp. 11–42.
• — (1941), "Patterns and Problems of Development" provide the foundation in biology for Wheeler's thought.
35 Wheeler (1929), Chapter VI, "Emotive Behavior", pp. 161–162, notes both Darwin and Lamarck as representative of opposing theories of evolution which raise further questions about the origin of emotional and instinctive responses.
• Cannon (1958), Chapter IV, "Lamarckism", pp. 60–78, provides a concise overview of Lamarckian ideas, related "laws" and criticism.
36 Some of the "modern biologists" to whom Wheeler refers have already been cited in previous notes especially the work of Coghill. The frame of reference within which Wheeler was working on the problem of human development and learning included the work of Coghill, Child, and Jennings who undertook their research and writing primarily during the first quarter of the twentieth century.

organism grows these structures under these laws, deposits them. It takes the energy it gets from whatever source; mothers, in mammals before it is born, get their energy from the mother's bloodstream or from air or whatever and it converts its energy and lays it down and deposits it under certain laws. Heredity doesn't tell it which way to go. Here's another thing. There was a turtle born out here a few months ago with two perfect heads. It was pictured in *Life and Look* magazine and those two heads functioned perfectly and when you feed one head, the other head doesn't know that what one head eats goes to the same place. It doesn't know that so it fights for any food. One will seize it out of the jaws of the other fellow not knowing.

Wheeler and these scientists had been, as Wheeler points out, influenced by the work of Jean-Baptiste Lamarck, a late eighteenth and early nineteenth century French scientist. Lamarck (1744–1829) studied and undertook research in the areas of natural history, zoology, meteorology, physical science and geology. He developed a broad theory of evolution, however; he seems most commonly to be associated with only one facet of that theory, the inheritance of acquired characteristics. This theory is, of course, antithetical to Darwin's concept of natural selection and Mendal's genetic theory. Packard (1901) points out that the work Lamarck and his *Philosophie Zoologie* (1809) was passed over by the community of scientists in Lamarck's time as Darwin's theory of evolution based on the concept of the survival of the fittest became recognized as the mainstream scientific position.

Packard identified a renewal of interest in Lamarckism in Europe and especially in America with the publication of Herbert Spencer's Principles of Biology, (1896) Vol. I, Chapter VII, "How Organic Evolution is Caused", pp. 403–410. Further, Packard cites books, reports, and proceedings of scientific meetings in which "upwards of forty working biologists, many of whom were brought up, so to speak, in the Darwinian faith, to show the pendulum of evolutionary thoughts is swinging away from the narrow and restricted conception of natural selection, pure and simple, as the sole or most important factor, and returning in the direction of Lamarckism". Wheeler's declaration of his debt to Lamarck is better understood within this context and an appreciation of Wheeler's optimistic view of the potential for the improvement of the human condition. See Wheeler Interview, pp. 103–104. Further, the Neo-Lamarckian position undergirds Wheeler's discussion contained here on pp. 83–85.

Lamarck and his theory becomes an interesting focus of study when seen in the context of the Darwinian evolutionary, Lamarckian, and Mendalian genetic theory controversy. During his lifetime he had touch with many of the major intellectual and scientific figures of his day. Admired by some,

R.W.H. What is the whole in this?

R.H.W. Good question. The turtle is the whole. It's no worse a problem than if you had an extra finger or something. It's still a whole; there are two separate brains. Yes, but they are both integrated with the same body in the sense that it's a whole, but here's the point I'm coming to, namely that heredity didn't determine the fact that it had two heads. Neither parent had two heads. Those two heads came about due to accident in this

---

attacked and/or ignored by others, his failure to obtain recognition in his own time proved to be a source of bitterness for him. He died blind and in poverty, cared for by his daughter, and was buried in an unmarked common grave. Packard (1901) provides as detailed as possible account of his life and work. His chapter on Neo-lamarckians provides some helpful data for an understanding of Wheeler's "modern scientists". Originally printed in 1901, the biography was reprinted by Arno Press in 1980.

• Burkhardt (1977), *The Spirit of the System Lamarck and Evolutionary Biology*, provides a readable and well documented treatment of Lamarck and his work from the perspective of a modern historian of science. If the reader were to choose but one book to extend his/her study of Lamarck, though not geared specifically to the study of learning, it would prove to be a rewarding choice.

Lamarck's name, to the detriment of his reputation and to the disappoint-ment of the Neo-Lamarckians, became associated with two unfortunate inci-dents in the twentieth century, the Kammerer and the Lysenko incidents. Paul Kammerer appeared to have falsified research findings he developed to support the principle of the inheritance of acquired characteristics during his research on the midwife toad. (Koestler 1971). Kammerer's suicide in 1926 seemed to uphold the accusation of wrongdoing.

Lysenko, who embraced Lamarckian principles as supportive of the goals of the Soviet Union's agricultural policy as well as social policy, directed Soviet science from the 1930's to the 1960's. His influence brought about the destruction of genetics in the Soviet Union. Burkhardt (1977), p. 3, Joravsky, (1970), Gillespie, (1950), and Medvedev, (1969), provide additional data re-lating to the episode.

Three works, Cannon (1958), (1959), (1957), provide a spirited defence of Lamarck's theories in the light of the criticisms of the Darwinian evolution-ists and the traditional geneticists. It is interesting to note that these exposi-tions and defences of Lamarck's work were written close to the time of the Wheeler interview. The writers do not know whether Wheeler was aware of the publication of these books when he spoke of others' interest in Lamarck.

Gould (1991) in a series of essays, discusses the biological, historical and social influences from this controversy.

engineering of growth. Now the accident was a distortion of a gradient of energy. Now, I didn't go into that and I haven't time to go into that, but gradients determine a lot of the details of growth. It tells you which is your head end and which is your tail end. It determines how many heads. If we were to stop the gradient we would get an extra head. If we manufacture two peaks to the gradient instead of one, as you should have, you get two heads. In fact, you can get almost as many heads as you want by multiplying the peaks of the gradient.

R.W.H.   So individual differences aren't due so much to heredity as to the laws of growth?

R.H.W.   Right.

R.W.H.   The laws of growth. There are three factors: the laws of heredity, the laws of growth and environment.

R.H.W.   Right. You take my rats. Why, this is why I am a Lamarckian, not a Darwinian. Those rats, hot and cold rats were brothers and sisters when they were weaned. They came from the same litter. They had the same heredity. They were moved into two rooms – one at 90° one at 60°.

<Tape change>

Why Ray, we were on the question of heredity and I just mentioned that I thought the Lamarckian point of view was superior to Darwinian when it comes to evolution and heredity and here's why these rats I started to tell you about they all had the same heredity.

They were – separated into three environments: hot, medium and cold – came out very differently physically right from the start. The first generation moved into these rooms when they were three weeks old and just weaned, developed entirely different structures. Well, they still were rats, but the hot rats living in high outside temperatures grew elongated bodies, longer tails when compared to the length of the bodies, longer bodies, long narrow bodies, narrow head cases, small brains capacity, long noses, big ears. They were expanding in adjustment to environment, their radiation surface making it easier for them to get rid of the body heat which they were constantly generating and due to the high outside temperature could get rid of only with difficulty. As it was, they had to slow down in all their behavior, all their physiology and activity not to generate heat they couldn't get rid of – otherwise they would develop a fever and die.

But the point is this – these animals in the hot room changed their bodies, their measurements and the functioning of their internal organs. Their glands were slower, their movements were slower. Everything about them. Their hearts were slower. They changed themselves in this adjustment process. As I told my students, effort counts. They did it. It wasn't done for them. They did the work of shaping up these changed structures in response to the difference in the environment. Now the germ plasm was effected at the same time. It obviously was and for two reasons. One is the offspring had the same pattern of measurement right off. Only one generation. It doesn't take long. The germ plasm was effected other ways. They were unstable from the very, very beginning. They were far less fertile. The germ plasm was many ways defective. Both sexes were not as fertile. Anywhere near the first generation. In the hot room at 90° (the rats) had two families a year, spring and fall. The second generation only had one a year. The third generation – half of them had none. The fourth generation, they were all sterile. We had to replenish the population of the hot room constantly from the control room.

On the other hand, the cold rats, brothers and sisters of the hot rats, had five litters a year, more than the normal rats and big healthy litters. Their bodies both adults and offspring were chunky. They were thick, heavy bones, shorter tails, smaller ears and everything pointed to the contraction of body surface in order that radiation would be slower because outside temperatures were cold. They were conserving. Now those changes occurred at once and remained. That's what made me a Lamarckian. The animals did it themselves. Now all these objections to the Lamarckian theory against the inheritance of acquired characteristics seem to me to be very stupid because the objections were all artificial. We talk about cutting off mices' tails for generations on end and they are still born with tails. Well, the animals didn't shorten their tails, the animals didn't cut off their own tails; it is purely an artificial thing.[37]

---

37 Wheeler (1946), "Climate and Human Behavior" in the *Encyclopaedia of Psychology*, pp. 80–81, contains reports of studies undertaken by researchers at several universities exploring the topic. A study by Dr Clarence A. Mills at the University of Cincinnati Medical School dealt with mice bred under artificial climates which demonstrated the influence of temperature on conditioning, size, body form and fertility.

• — (1931), Chapter III, "Biological Organization" pp. 67–82. Although the pages cited do not treat the rat studies described in the interview, the material dealing with the "laws of nature" particularly in relation to whole as determi-

The sheep breeders have been cutting off the tails of sheep for countless generations and yet they are still born with tails as long as ever. Well the sheep didn't shorten their own tails. Now, Lamarck[38] inferred that if the animal makes the change itself through its own effort and if the change is of survival value it is inherited. If it is of survival value, it simply means that the germ plasm changed with it somewhat. And we know that germ plasm is effected by the same set of conditions that effect the body. That's what makes me a Lamarckian.

R.W.H. So that there is a relationship between the laws of growth and the laws of heredity but they are separate and distinct things in your view.

R.H.W. Right. You can't divorce the two from each other. They cooperate. They work together and produce an organism. You can't have an organism unless you have both. There'd be no organism.

As Jennings[39] in one of his books said, theoretically, it is possible to produce a variation in a species or a new species by holding the germ plasm constant and altering the environment enough. You eventually get a new species, a new variety or you can do it the other way: hold the animal constant and manipulate the germ plasms. Either way will get you the same results which simply points to the fact that you can't have one without the other.

---

nants of parts, provides a background of information which assists understanding of the material discussed in this segment of the interview.

38 Cannon (1958), Chapter IV, pp. 62–72. Cannon provides an exposition and discussion of Lamarck's position.
   Packard (1901), Chapter XVI, "The Steps in the Development of Lamarck's View on Evolution Before the Publication of His *Philosophie Zoologique*", pp. 232–278, and Burkhardt (1977), Chapter 6, "Invertebrate Zoology and the Inspiration of Lamarck's Evolutionary Views", pp. 143–185.

39 Wheeler (1929), Chapter V, "Intelligent Behavior: Direct Methods", pp. 118–119, cites Jenning's study with paramecia in opposition to tropism theory.
 • — (1932), Chapter I, "Point of View", p. 15, and Chapter IX, "The Source of Intelligent Behavior", p. 173, include works by H.S. Jennings in their bibliographies. Chapter I cites H.S. Jennings, (1920) *Suggestions of Modern Science Concerning Education*, and Chapter IX cites H.S. Jennings, (1930) *The Biological Basis of Human Nature*. Pages 163–166 of this chapter provide information about germ plasm, conditions influencing changes in the germ plasm as well as heredity.

R.W.H. Could we move on to a new thing?

R.H.W. Yes.

R.W.H. Would you talk quite specifically about the learning process? How does learning take place? Learning has been involved in all of the things that we have discussed but would you make a specific statement about it?

R.H.W. Yes, certainly. The learning process is a matter of development, a matter of growth, it is a matter of maturation. It is an unfolding, it is a development, but it is a series of discoveries, a series of emergences, a series of the developments of new capacities, new achievements. Let me give you an example.[40]

The child is in the first or second grade and he is being taught arithmetic and he is comes up with the equation. He is confronted with the equation of two plus two equals four. I don't care how many times the teacher repeats that. It won't mean a thing to that child until he is ready,[41] until the sounds will insight a growth process in that child's mind or his brain, I don't care which, so that the child will do something he has never done before in his life. He makes a discovery. The idea that two plus two equal four has to come into being in the child's mind as an invention

---

40 Here is Wheeler probing for meaning. He uses the words development, growth, maturation, unfolding, discovery, emergence, achievement. He uses these words not as literary metaphors and yet not as highly specific technical terminology. It becomes apparent that he has personal meaning for each of them, however. They are not synonymous.

- Wheeler (1929), Chapter IX, "Learning: Grosser Facts and Methods", pp. 239–267, encompasses many of the essential points which undergird Wheeler's position – goals, whole vs. parts, learning, pleasant and unpleasant experiences, tension, association and configuration.

- — (1930), Reading XIV, "How to Develop and Interest in One's Tasks and Work", pp. 255–257, contains an exposition of Wheeler's view of the learning process. Learning, discovery, interest and motivation are defined. Points of conflict with experience and association theory are identified.

41 This is the process of growth. The child will not grasp the insight until growth has occurred. It is not a matter of simple "readiness". Often in school the lesson moves on and individual children often miss "the window of opportunity".

exactly like the invention of an inventor, like the engineer or engineers who invented the airplane.[42]

By taking past experiences, neither of them like an airplane, but which insighted or stimulated this growth process, this advance in meaning or comprehension with the emergence of new ideas and new properties. For example, he may have read in his mind at one instant an electric motor propelling a fan, getting a breeze; the next instance he had in his mind a kite being suspended in the air. Well, how something akin to an explosion, a synthesis as having an emergent in his mind popped just like that. The concept came about through invention, through creative imagination of an airplane or something of that kind, a kite propelled by a motor. Now that is something new just as the meaning, two and two are four. The fact that it adds up to four is of necessity a discovery[43] on the part of that child's mind.[44]

R.W.H.   Could I interrupt a second?

R.H.W.   Yes.

R.W.H.   This discovery, this insight that he gains is unique in his own experience according to his own configuration so that two plus two equals

---

42 This phenomenon is very like that which he refers to as insight. It is to be presumed that he is describing the child grasping the concept of $2 + 2 = 4$, and not just relating the sound of the words as he suggests in line 4. It is interesting how he passes over making critical distinction between mind and brain. Discovery, p. 41 line 42, seems very like what others would simply call learning. The idea of *invention* in this case seems somewhat puzzling and not paralleling the process he describes in the next paragraph.

43 A *discovery*, but not quite the same as *invention*.

• Wheeler (1931), Chapter VI, "The Laws of Learning", pp. 141–177, is an exposition of the organismic view of learning. Included in the chapter are such topics as instinct, learning by doing, practice, insight, memory, meaning as well as a summary of the laws of learning. A criticism of associationism is included.

44 It is in this section of the interview where he is drawn back to reconsider things that were at the forefront of his interest in the early 1930's. One can see why Wheeler and Perkins (1933) was the psychology of the Progressive Education Movement. These ideas of maturation, perception, insight, growth, readiness, provided the psychological rationale for progressive teaching that was unavailable in the connectionist psychology of Thorndike.

four for him is not exactly the same as two plus two for four equals four for the teacher.

R.H.W. Oh, yes. Most certainly it's the same. It is the same logic. It has to be. It isn't another number. It isn't five or three or any fraction thereof, it's four. The meaning is the same and can be communicated and if they want to prove it to each other, then let them count out four blocks or four of anything. They will agree on it. It is absolutely a comparable thing.[45] Now there is a difference in the certainty of it. There is a difference in the security and the security connection with it, but that is something else.

R.W.H. I am sorry I interrupted you.

R.H.W. No, glad you did. Well that's what I mean. Learning is a succession of inventions which we call the growth of insight, the growth of understanding, the growth of intelligence and it is anything but mechanical. It is anything but conditioned. The only place in the picture where conditioning comes in is the stimulus has to be there to challenge the person to stir him up, put him in a state of imbalance, whatever you want to call it, so that he'll go to work so that he will apply his own energy along the line of development of some kind.[46]

---

45 But a comparable thing is not an identical thing.
- Wheeler (1932), Chapter XIII, "Analysis of the Learning Process: Maturation, Goal, Insight", pp. 239–259, provides a thorough introduction to the concepts introduced in this section of the interview. Chapters XIII through XX deal with various aspects of the learning process.
- — (1940), Chapter VIII, "Learning – General Problems", deals with most of the issues raised in this segment of the interview.

46 It seems to the interviewers that the result is the same whether the process result is called insight or learning. The distinction may be in the idea that Wheeler has overreached his own dictum. In the case of insight, there may have been numerous smaller stimulus–response interactions inclusive within that which he deems to call invention or insight. In the process of *discovery*, that $2 + 2 = 4$, one must conceptualize 2, the meaning of plus, the meaning of equal, and the idea of 4. There are innumerable micro-interactions of learning prior to the insight of one 2 together with a second 2 total or comprise 4.
- Wheeler (1932), Chapter V, "Evolution of the Learning Process", pp. 79–80, discusses the laws of learning and their application to both humans and animals.

Now I don't care what the kind of learning is, whether it is intellectual or muscular, it is the same thing.[47]

Now there is another important aspect I think is very, very important. Now we come back to these organismic laws. Namely that in learning, in principle logically, it is the whole that is laying down or precipitating or developing a part. Now that sounds very vague and very abstract but let me explain what I mean by reference to muscular maturation. I go back to the work of Coghill[48] and others where they show that mass action comes first.[49] Now, you can't suppose by any stretch of the imagination that little bits of movements, reflexes or something equivalent that occur at first as separate energies ever get put together. Coordination isn't a matter of putting pieces together. It is a matter of individuating or differentiating specialized movements from previously existing mass actions. You have read Coghill's work on *Anatomy and the Problem of Behavior*. That's the story.

I always use the illustration of wiggling your ears when you come to this. Can you wiggle your ears, Ray?

R.W.H. No, I can't.

---

47 This is an important notion overlooked in the consideration of learning, that learning can refer to any kind of behavior; cognitive, affective or psychomotive and that, in turn, behavior is usually values driven and that valuing provide the stimuli Wheeler describes above for the motivation of action. It may be that the relationship of values as stimuli toward behavioral action provides the key element in so-called values teaching. Values consideration must be related to stimulating new behavior, toward learning insight and intelligence in human and perhaps other organisms. This knowledge provides vital clues for the development of teaching strategies in the classroom. Behavior is values driven.

48 Coghill (1929), Lecture I, "The Development of Behavior and its Anatomical Explanation in a Typical Vertebrate", pp. 36–38, and Lecture III, "Growth of the Nerve Cell and Interpretation of Behavior", pp. 86–89.

49 Ledbetter (1991), p. 107. All golf swing theory focuses on the fact that mass action leads and controls individual action and confirms Wheeler's idea of individuation and differentiation. No amount of manipulation of small movement can compensate for faulty mass action initiation. This is illustrated in students learning to drive a motor car. Insight with respect to driving only occurs when driving is done – not when gear changing, wheel turning, braking are practised as individual exercises.

R.H.W. Well, if you tried as I get my students to do in front of the class to demonstrate this, if you try hard enough in order to find these muscles at the base of the ear which are really residual organs, they are vestidual organs, they're dying. They are in the process of disappearing in the course of evolution. We don't wiggle our ears. We are not donkeys. So in order to find them they have to contract all the musculature around the scalp, the face, even the neck. Then, after that, if they are alert enough they can begin to feel the muscles at the base of the ear as second sensations. Not only can they begin to do that, then they can wiggle their ears but as long as they wiggle their ears, no matter how skilled they get, they first have to tense their face, tense their scalp to find those muscles.

You will never see a baby cry who isn't squirming. Why, they have to squirm to find their voice. These salamanders have to curl their body first one way then another in order to move their legs. So that when the legs are first moved as separate parts of the body they're still moved as part of a curling movement. First one side, then the other. The legs are coordinated by virtue of differentiation from an already coordinated movement. Mass action. So that the contraction curls the body one way will contract that leg from the action that curls the body the other way will contract the other leg timing the legs in relation to each other.[50] In other words, the whole times the parts, they can't be turned any other way. They can't be turned any other way. There are more mechanisms that can time movements in relation to each other except through mass action. That is why you have to assume a posture. If you are going to dive, you have to assume a posture. If you are going to swing and hit the ball at golf, that posture[51] is necessary before you can time a movement against your wrist, time your shoulder or what not. The whole comes first, that is an organismic law and it controls the parts. Just the opposite of conditioning.

---

50 It is interesting to watch the behavior of orchestra conductors such as Zubin Mehta as they operate off mass action as initiation to teasing particular subtleties of performance from orchestra members. Sometimes the more subtle the sought response, the broader the action of the conductor.

51 This concept of mass action certainly is widely supported in golf tutoring. Every method of golf instruction conceived of the mass action of larger muscles setting everything else in motion culminating in the smooth effortless powerful golf swing.

• Wheeler (1932), Chapter XIV, "Analysis of the Learning Process: Coordination and Motivation", pp. 265–269, relates Snoddy's analysis of movement to patterned movements in golf. Most frequently cited is G.E. Coghill, (1929),

R.W.H. Just the opposite.

R.H.W. Just the opposite of conditioning. Getting the part from the whole instead of getting the whole from the part.[52]

R.W.H. How does memory and forgetting come in? I know you have made reference to it but would you like to elaborate on it?

R.H.W. Well, I am so unorthodox that I don't even ask you to believe me, but it is fun to go over this.[53] Of course, I don't believe in the old fashioned trace theory of memory anyway. You have been up in your

---

and Reading XXVII, "The Early Development of Behavior in Amblystoma and in Man", by Coghill in Wheeler (1930).

- — (1931), Chapter IV, "The Development of Behavior", pp. 111–112, discusses coordinated movement and cues in infants.

- — (1930), Reading XVI, "The Role of Form in Learning", pp. 289–295. In these more extensively developed notes to Gifford's "Role of Form in Learning", Wheeler reviews material covered in prior editor's notes encompassing learning and the organismic laws with illustrative material.

- — (1940), Introduction, pp. 18–26, relates to the "primacy of the wholes".

52 This would seem to be essence of it. The idea is clear enough in itself, but whether it is a model of the learning process is something else again.

- — (1930), Reading XXVII, "The Early Development of Behavior in Amblystoma and in Man", pp. 528–531 combines a consideration of the "eight organismic laws applied to the nervous system" and the findings of Coghill to provide a base for an understanding of the idea that "... the growth of parts within the whole is throughout a process of reaching remote ends established by pre-existing gradients."

- — (1931), Chapter III, "Biological Organization", pp. 70–71, introduces Wheeler's concept of the universal laws of nature. Identifying eight laws, he presents them in relation to physical and biological problems, pp. 71–94. The major portion of the text is an "application" of the same basic laws to the problems of human nature, chapters IV through VII. Chapter II, "The Transition to Scientific Psychology", describes in detail the contrast between a mechanistic view of psychology with a more "vitalistic" view. Wheeler identifies an alternative to these "dead-end" positions, the organic whole, pp. 62–66. Complexity and wholeness are discussed pp. 64–66.

- — (1940), Introduction, pp. 16–26, provides an extended discussion of the concepts related to the primacy of wholes and origins of parts.

53 At the time of the interview, the writers had no idea that the questions were about ideas that Wheeler had been concerned with some thirty years earlier.

room, I know, and you have decided, well I am going back down. I am going down to the kitchen to get something, you go down and you forget what you went down there for. In order to recall what it was you had in mind you go back to your room. You can't recall until you do go back to the situation in which you generated the idea or goal in the first place. Well, memory is an incomplete re-creation. It isn't a recall. It is an incomplete re-creation of a previous experience if and when you have confronted with enough similarity in the stimulus pattern to generate it. There is no trace necessary at all. It is just re-creation. Now you have the same experience in long latent memory. You have forgotten something for years, years and years, like the oldest living alumnus of Dartmouth. Remember that story?

R.W.H. No.

R.H.W. He was 94 years old or something like that and he always lived alone.[54] He was feted and greatly made of and he went back to a reunion at commencement time and he was given this banquet in his honor and, in the excitement, back in the old hall where he orated, where he had a speech course called, "oratory" or "elocution" when he was a freshman, back in the same hall with the same paintings on the wall, everything – same panelling, he thought of one of his old freshman orations, recited it verbatim. Now that was 75 years after.

I have had similar experiences on a less remarkable scale, being able to recall things long since forgotten, when I return to the same environment where you get the same stimulation in the first place. Memory to me isn't recalling a trace but it is a re-creation of an experience, not completely, because you don't repeat the situation completely.

Now we have one means of recreating original situations without going back to them physically. There is language. Here is the nearest I come to the behaviorist.[55] Here we have a large part of our previous environments still existing symbolically in our language. So we think of those words like vacation or mountains or Mt. Shasta or what not, it takes us back there.

---

54 Wheeler and Perkins (1932), Chapter XXI, "The Problem of Memory", pp. 396–397. The "old Grad" story is recounted within the context of a consideration of the law of configuration.

55 Wheeler (1929), Chapter X, "Learning Behavior – The More Precise Facts and Methods", pp. 269–300 deals with Wheeler's theory of memory forgetting and related issues which are closely aligned with the interview.

R.W.H.   Suppose that you just mouthed it without verbalizing. No?

R.H.W.   Yes, definitely, sure. It doesn't have to be audible, but I don't think you can think of a word without wiggling your tongue or your voice muscles.

R.W.H.   This is the same as getting poised for a dive.

R.H.W.   Exactly.

R.W.H.   You were saying earlier that insight is the same as intelligence. I am wondering how you would measure intelligence in this case. How would you tell whether or not a person is intelligent?

R.H.W.   Achievement.[56] There is nothing in this world that can be measured that isn't action of some kind. Anything on the order of a potential is never measured. The only thing you can measure is action. It is kinetic energy and not any potential energy. Potential energy, as I understand it, doesn't have identity, anyway. Its a specific form of motion that has no identity if its purely potential anyway. It can't.

- — (1931), Chapter VI, "The Laws of Learning", pp. 166–179, provides further discussion as well as a variety of examples of the organismic conception of memory.
- — (1932), Chapter XXI, "The Problems of Memory", pp. 385–407, treats all of the issues related to memory introduced in the interview. Trace theory as well as alternative theories of memory are discussed. The problem of forgetting is examined. Suggestions for more effective patterns of high school and college study are provided.
- — (1940), Chapter IX, "Learning – The More Precise Facts and Methods", pp. 238–244, deals with the problem of memory from an organismic point of view.
- 56 In one word, Wheeler (see Skinner Interview, pp. 57–58) is clearly in agreement with the behaviorists. Is not achievement very close to the answer that Skinner would give, "changed behavior"? Which suggests, of course, that all intelligence tests are really achievement texts, that achievement tests are intelligence tests, that *all* tests are achievement tests, that all tests, then, are intelligence tests. It also suggests that both so–called intelligence tests and achievement tests are seeking to find out how well individuals can perform on predetermined particular kinds of tasks. It would seem to explain why most tests given are biased against any whose opportunity to achieve in favoured

Here is an example of that. You see, Ray, psychologists try to get away with so much stuff. If you let me, there are some educators included in that group who make mistakes. Their thinking is just because they haven't had a logical training.

R.W.H. We were talking about measuring and you said you can only measure ...

R.H.W. Right. For example, white light does not contain colored light within it in the form in which we see it. Red and blue and green and violet don't exist within white light with the identity that they have when you see them as colors. In fact, that identity is lost. So you can't measure the colored light under the white light at all. You can't get to it. You can't get to potential energy. You can't measure it. You can't get to native endowment to measure it if you worked a thousand years. It doesn't have any identity. There is no such thing then as measuring native endowment.

---

areas of experience is never tested. This is the key to bias against so called minorities in standard tests. Tests are constructed with the assumption that those unacquainted with dominant cultural values are without culture. Tests seldom are constructed which seek to assess mastery of so called "sub" cultural value behaviors. Is a child highly skilled in subcultural language mastery (slang, vulgarity, profanity, specialised ethnic or class usage) less intelligent than a child with mastery of a more "culturally refined" vocabulary?

Skinner indicated earlier (p. 58) that tests seek to determine what students do not know rather than what they do know. While it is apparent that some will have attended to little experience valued by test writers, precious few have attended to nothing at all. They have very possibly achieved at extremely high levels in areas that testers would not think to measure or perhaps be embarrassed to measure. One is reminded of J.M. Barrie's play, *The Admirable Crichton* (1928) where the butler is king on the desert island, but the master is restored to superior status upon returning to a more rationalized cultural context. Levels of achievement may extend across the widest range of behavior and include feeling and attitude as well as understanding, knowledge and psychomotion.

- Wheeler (1940), Chapter VI, "Intelligent Behavior – Indirect Methods", discusses methods of studying intelligent behavior with special focus on intelligence quotient, levels of performance as well as statistical procedures for interpreting test data. Pages 166–170 address the "nature/nurture problem": pp. 171–173 treat topics mentioned in the interview – native capacity, work

R.W.H. It is a part of the whole, though.

R.H.W. It is there. It is there potentially. You cannot measure it. The only way you can measure intelligence is to measure achievement and that is the only way you can define intelligence is what you can do, now what you are doing under the circumstances.[57]

Now intelligences can vary. Actually it varies from day to day. It isn't constant and all this tommyrot about children born with an IQ just so much and no more is all tommyrot. There is nothing to it. I know I sound dogmatic,[58] but, for heaven's sake, if you only knew a little of this logic I am talking about you wouldn't make these mistakes of interpretation.

---

equated with achievement. Constancy of the IQ is discussed on pp. 173–175. This material includes references to the study of twins by Newman, Freeman, and Holzinger.

- Gould, (1981), *The Mismeasure of Man*, Chapter 5, "The Hereditarian Theory of I.Q.: An American Invention", provides an alternative view of I.Q. and its measurement as well as an alternative context for examination of the concept and of practice.

57 Which is the behaviorist position, "What you can do (that is, can do now) ... is change behavior".

- Wheeler (1932), Chapter IX, "The Source of Intelligent Behavior" pp. 166–172, discusses achievement as kinetic energy, constancy of IQ, intelligence of adopted children as well as heredity and environment. Further, Chapter X, "The Measurement of Intelligence", pp. 174–197, explores intelligence tests, statistical procedures and the interpretation of test results. Chapter XXVI, "New Procedures in Education", pp. 495–513, reviews some of the developments in the education measurement movement which emerged in the 1920s and early 1930s. Wheeler discusses these developments within the context of the then evolving student-centered school. Chapter XXVI does not, in all respects, impinge directly on the content of the interview. It is of interest to anyone concerned about the implications of Wheeler's thinking for classroom instruction.

- — (1940), Chapter IV, "Intelligent Behavior: Indirect Methods:, pp. 166–179, includes the following topics: The Nature of Inheritance, Limitations of Inheritance, Relativity of Inheritance, The Function of Environment, The Function of Education in Relation to Heredity, The Problem of Intelligence and Further Misconceptions of Intelligence.

58 One would never accuse Wheeler of lacking passion. It is his passion that leads to his undoing.

Now the reason why Terman[59] and others found what they thought was the constancy of an IQ in children, was simply due to the fact their environment was the same.

These kids grew up under the same circumstances, in the same home with the same amount of challenge, the same amount of opportunity. That is why identical twins come out so much alike because they have the same environment, not only because they have the same heredity.[60]

---

59 Terman (1916), *The Measurement of Intelligence.*
* — (1928), "The Influence of Nature and Nurture Upon Intelligence Scores", *Educational Psychology*, pp. 362–373.
* Wheeler (1929), Chapter IV, "Intelligent Behavior: Indirect Methods", pp. 87–115, contains a review of methods of studying intelligence, the use of test results and their interpretation.; pp. 107–115 are of particular interest to readers of this interview as the material contained touches upon constancy of intelligence, training, inheritance, as well as pacing.
* — (1931), Chapter VI, "The Laws of Learning", p. 141. "There is no activity of man from birth to death that does not depend upon a growth potential; nor is there any activity that does not depend upon environment, for growth potential exists only with reference to environment."
60 Wheeler's confidence in the importance of both heredity and environment in the determination of intelligence is a question which contemporary researchers seem to find open and continue to pursue. The existence of data in which one could have confidence remains a stumbling block for those who seek precise determination of this issue for both identical and fraternal twins. Farber (1981), *Identical Twins Reared Apart: A Reanalysis*, offers a "survey and reanalysis of all published cases of identical twins reared apart." The research examines the nature nurture question through studies examined in the text. Farber's analysis of twin studies prior to 1981 reveal numerous flaws in the existing research methodology. Her work does point to the conclusion, however, that the more separated the twins were the more unlike their I.Q. In any event, the question of the proportional influence of environment and heredity on the development of intelligence requires further research. The text includes an extensive bibliography which would be most helpful in providing direction for further study. Osborne (1980), *Twins: Black and White*, presents an analysis of psychological test results and biometric measures of 496 pairs of black and white sets of twins. Analysis of personality, socioeconomic status, culture fair and primary mental ability tests and neurological findings are also reported. An extensive bibliography is also included.

Watson (1981), *Twins: An Uncanny Relationship?*, reports twin studies undertaken at the University of Minnesota and attempts through the studies to answer some of the questions raised by Farber. The text includes two

Now, separate these twins and they turn out very, very differently. If you give one opportunity and challenge and don't give the other one opportunity and challenge, they will deviate as any two children will deviate. Now, did you ever stop to think that in the same family no child has the same environment as any other child? Did you ever stop to think of that? A two year old sibling with four children, two, four, eight years of age. The environment of the two year old is that of all older children. The environment of the eight year old is that of all younger children. They don't have the same environment. They get different patterns of stimulation, all of them different in the family pattern. They are going to differentiate. They are going to be different individuals and they are not going to have the same intelligence although they presumably have had the same heredity.

R.W.H. You are convinced then that a child's potential could be destroyed by his environment.

R.H.W. Well, Ray, there isn't any use at all in talking about it. It doesn't mean anything. The only thing it can possibly mean is what it means in mathematics and what it means in physics. You've got to have source (sic) from which energy comes and that's all there is to it.

You can't talk about the amount. It is fruitless to talk about the amount. You don't know what the amount is. The only kind of energy that can be measured in any amount is action. Kinetic energy is achievement and you examine that and give a mental test. It is the achievement that you are measuring and not the native endowment. Now that achievement may be high today and lower tomorrow.

Look at those hundreds of high school graduates who took the college entrance examination in Amherst. Huntington[61], the Yale geographer, tells about it. They all took this test just a few hours before a hurricane struck and it was very hot and humid and they were very depressed. Well, the average score was way below the expected, way below normal for the

---

chapters, "The Science of Coincidence", and "Coincidences Around the World" which help to put the task of identifying differences and similarities in perspective.

61 Wheeler describes the work of Ellsworth Huntington of Yale in his article, "Climate and Human Behavior" in the *Encyclopaedia of Psychology*, (1946). He also includes a list of Huntington's works relating to the influence of climate on human behavior.

entire group. The next day another group of several hundred took the examination in the same place and the barometer changed and it was cool and clear and not depressing and they went as far above the average – they went above the average as the first group went below. There you are. They are more intelligent one day than another. It just means nothing to say that their innate endowment was the same both days. It doesn't mean a thing. It doesn't help understand it or anything.

R.W.H. This is an optimistic point of view.[62] Isn't it?

R.H.W. Certainly, because if you are convinced as a teacher, especially if you are teaching little children, that it is the opportunity you give them that is more important than any such thing as native endowment, then if you do have a moron or a borderline case, you will, regardless of its cause, you will be more willing and anxious to do something for that child. You

---

62 Obviously both Skinner and Wheeler, as essentially environmentalists, are committed to the nurture side of the nature-nurture question. In saying that, this is optimistic, the interviewers are being optimistically one-sided, for the fact remains that while it suggests that nearly all children may have an unknowable potential which may well be developed, all children also have to live in public and private environments of such diversity that luck emerges as the more important element in the development of individual intelligence as any single factor even when the genetic history of the child is eliminated as the critical factor. Sociobiologists, Wilson (1978), would be in total disagreement, of course.

In each generation the nature-nurture controversy is renewed. Hernestein and Murray (1994), Rushton (1994), and Itzkoff (1994), are recent entries. All make the case that intelligence is heritable and express concern that there is downward pressure on intelligence as the population at the lower end of an intelligence scale are reproducing at a greater rate. All three books posit a resultant two class stressed society. It was but little more than a decade ago in *The Mismeasure of Man* that Steven Jay Gould (1981) concluded that "determinist arguments for ranking people according to a single scale of intelligence, no matter how numerically sophisticated, have recorded little more than social prejudice."

There is another factor which, unfortunately, is seldom taken into account when considering children's behavior, that is biochemical, electromagnetic and other physiological conditions acting on the behavior of organisms; some of which may be in the genetic history and some perhaps resulting from organic changes acquired in the post natal history of the organism.

don't consider him absolutely hopeless.[63] Like a child I knew once. He was twelve years old and had a mental age of eight, that makes him an imbecile, high grade imbecile. Two years after medical treatment and diet and specialized education, stimulation, they tested him again when he was fourteen and he had a mental age of twelve. In other words, he gained four years in mental age while he was growing two years. That is an authentic case. There are lots of them so it does help to try.[64]

If you say, well, this poor child is helpless, he has inherited an IQ of 80, he can't get any more no matter what you do. All you can do is to teach him to spin threads or weave brooms.

R.W.H. You don't believe in adjusting to what seems inevitable but ...

R.H.W. Rather trying to stimulate, trying to improve, trying to elevate, definitely.

---

63 • Wheeler (1932), Chapter I, "The Point of View", pp. 10–14, reviews "changing conceptions of nature" and changes in psychology which suggest an altered role and perspective for teachers. The reading reflects some of the optimism embedded in the closing segment of the interview. Chapter IX, "The Source of Intelligent Behavior", p. 166, comments briefly on the "function of education in relation to heredity."

• — (1940), Chapter VI, "Intelligent Behavior: Indirect Methods", p. 178, notes the importance of educational environment in the development of intelligence.

• — (1935), "A Set of Postulates for Educational Theory I. The Background", *Journal of Educational Research*, pp. 321–333 and "Postulates for a Theory of Education II. A Methodology for Educational Research", *Journal of Educational Research*, November 1935, pp. 187–195. These articles present a discussion of the possibility of improvement in education within the context of mechanistic and vitalistic cycles of social and intellectual history. Wheeler points out that "... it becomes clear that scientific and social progress have been the outcome of a strikingly universal and unified pattern of thought, a universal logic or point of view." The vitalist point of view provides a positive context for social and educational improvement.

64 Lane and Stratford (1985), *Current Approaches to Down's Syndrome*, reports the efforts of the Down's Children's Association to bring together the findings of researchers in the field with a consideration of the relevance of these studies "for the wellbeing of those with Down's Syndrome". The text chapters deal with the many facets of Down's Syndrome – The Social and Historical Context, Physical Aspects, Educational Aspects, and Life Chances.

R.W.H. Would you reinforce that for us? You haven't written much about these things recently. Have your ideas changed much since you were more active in this field?

R.H.W. No. As far as my own thinking is concerned I think I am more entrenched in it now than I was 25 years ago. I have seen it confirmed so many times. It was borne out so many times, but, then I am more of a nonconformist now than when I was younger.

R.W.H. Do you think that your ideas and your writings had something to do with what some describe as life adjustment?[65]

R.H.W. I don't know. I should hope so. I imagine it has done a little. I would like to add that phrase "life adjustment" to creative adjustment.[66]

The issues raised by Wheeler in this interview are specifically dealt with in Chapter 10, "The Development of Intelligence". Lane and Stratford suggest that studies dealing with intelligence quotient from the 1940s to mid-1980s are seriously out of date. The most important recent developments reflect the growth of early intervention programs. The writers report that despite some methodological problems, there is a near-unanimity of opinion that the outcomes are positive and that the early intervention programs "are conferring real benefit to the children in raising their overall I.Q. levels at least in the short term, although it has not been unequivocally established that they also prevent the usual I.Q. decline." (pp. 183–184)

A study by Rhodes *et al* (1969) reports an early intervention program which included the teaching of reading. The findings of this report reveal a study of seriously retarded children who "in 2.5 years, changed from essentially non-verbal youngsters communicating only through bodily gestures and inarticulate sounds, to children with a relatively small but very usable expressive vocabulary, the ability to comprehend a number of basic concepts to read and enjoy simple books", p. 317. In any event, a perusal of the studies in the text provide support for Wheeler's position relative to the variability of ability to learn among Down's Syndrome children as well as the unresolved nature of many questions dealing with the nurture of these children.

65 This question, when asked, had a somewhat negative connotation. It referred to what seemed a bland concept of normative educational goals which distorted and diminished the so-called progressive movement.

66 The interviewers remain impressed with Wheeler's optimism. He seemed confident in the potential of education as an interventional strategy for change in children's prospects.

*B.F. Skinner at the colloquim at Rhode Island College, Providence, R.I., USA, in 1981.
Others in the photograph are (l.–r.): R.W. Houghton, M.T. Lapan and L.E. Alfonso.*

III. Comparison of Views

What is to be made of these interviews, these conversations on learning and intelligence? The writers had approached the task with five basic questions.

1. What is the nature of personkind?
2. What are intelligence and individual differences?
3. How do organisms, especially human organisms, learn?
4. What is memory? Why do people forget?
5. How is learning to be evaluated?

Hilgard (1948) had committed to the idea that learning theory fell into two classes based on the broad notion that learning tended to be holistic, that is, occurring from wholes to parts or atomistic, parts to wholes. It was originally assumed that Skinner, the radical behaviorist, was atomistic and that Wheeler, the organismist, was holistic. Hilgard continued to use the atomistic/holistic dichotomy through Editions II (1956) and III (1962) of *Theories of Learning*. Hilgard and Bower (1966) ceased using this form or organisation. Wheeler was eliminated, in any case.

In this section the writers will attempt to describe how each respondent in the 1959 interviews answered the questions.

SKINNER

1. *Nature of Personkind*

Skinner assumes that "we are only dealing with biology in a very broad sense". Further that ... "everything that man does is done by him as an organism with, of course, a genetic history and that people will differ very much as their genetic history differs and with a personal history."

He comments that most of his research (at that time) had been done with "so called lower animals" but with the assumption that there is nothing capricious about their behavior. He assumes their behavior to be regular and that tends to be confirmed in his experimental activity.

2. *Intelligence and Individual Differences*

In this interview Skinner, while not responding to a direct question, says that the "difference that turns up in work and teaching is the speed with which people can acquire a new behavior and how well they hold it." In other words, intelligence is judged on how quickly a person learns, and how long does he/she retain it. In some individuals the new learning/behavior slips away too quickly for it to be able to effect future behavior.

With reference to testing of intelligence he says, "... everything is in terms of observable behavior. You have no other information about people." "Individual differences are observable facts," Skinner says. They cannot be explained by saying that brains differ.

"No one has ever shown any correlation between behavioral property and a neurological one which would explain the so-called individual differences of an intellect or traits of character."

He goes on to say that individuals are born with different endowments, "... some capable of high development ... some probably not."

He strongly states that many seeming differences are merely the results of "... bad education or a bad environmental history", and that much difference is a matter of an individual merely having missed out on something in school or in his/her environment.

3. *Learning*

Skinner defines education/learning as change in behavior. "That's all it is and all it ever has been."

He sees the process of learning as occurring within an environment of interacting stimuli and responses, deliberate and indeliberate. Behavior changes as organisms responses to perceived stimuli in a contemporary environment are reinforced (rewarded) in a series of sequential operants in a direction toward new behavior.

This can be random or it can be directed. Control, that is the manipulated use of authority, is accomplished as responses desired (to the authority) occur. These initially small responses are immediately and positively reinforced. These small steps (operants) successively reinforced, move the respondants behavior in the direction of the desired behavior.

Skinner saw there to be no "freedom", for individuals as individuals are products of the contingencies of reinforcement in the life experience, and no dignity, in that credit could not be taken for behavior that could have been no other. (See Appendix D)

4. *Memory*

Skinner states in the interview, and confirms twenty years later, that he cannot manipulate the neurons in the brain of a person and hence, until he can do so, he is not interested in the inside of organisms in the sense of the nervous system and other internal mechanisms. This is not because they are not important, but because one cannot do much about them, especially in the living and intact organism.

He says that "... when I teach a child something today and discover that he knows it tomorrow that something survived overnight inside the child."

What survived is "... a changed child, a changed organism, partly in the brain and (he supposes) parts of the body." Such changes may have been different as a "... result of what happened to him yesterday."

The child is different and, in the observation of his behavior, the child still knows what he was taught yesterday. He says that if he knew how to use the "... storage mechanism" he would "... look into it, but (he) can't." All he claims to be able to do is "... put something in today and predict it will be there tomorrow and I can do that in light of my past experience." He would welcome information about brain physiology and would make

use of it, as available. He simply rejects dependence on what he terms "...
a conceptual nervous system, a nervous system that you would infer."

To appeal to these "phoney nervous systems hinders a "'lawful description of behavior.'"

5. *Evaluation*

In a Skinnerian educational system there would be no marks given. None
would be necessary as students would proceed through programs of instruction mastering each in turn for Skinner sees "everything in terms of
observable behavior. You have no other information about people."

"All tests come down to sampling behavior. Some sample it effectively,
some don't."

With a teaching machine, no tests are needed, he says. When a student
gets through the program of material there is no point in testing him. The
mark, if one insists on mark, would tell how far the student has proceeded.
It is to be assumed that records of students' progress would be in terms of
programs completed. When a program is completed Skinner says, "You
know it all then."

Work done is work done, it appears.

WHEELER

1. *Nature of Personkind*

Wheeler's answers to the writers' initial questions are interesting in the way he accepts their naïveté and covers them without hurting the dignity of the questioners. "Why, yes, Ray" he says, patronisingly "(people) are at the upper end of a biological continuum." He knows immediately that if the interviewer had prepared thoroughly, he would have known the wrong question had been asked.

Wheeler quickly goes on to make the question more sensible by saying that "... there is nothing basically different in principle between different levels of the animal kingdom in as far as the basic laws of their constitution are concerned." He then says, "... all organisms, from the simplest to the complex, obey or follow these organismic laws some part of which *you have in mind*." Wheeler was being polite, but, of course, the interviewer had failed to recognise the primacy of the laws.

In fact as he would later find out, the organismic laws have primacy in not only a biological continuum, but in matter, and in all things. The organismic laws in Wheeler's view eliminate the ancient dualism of mind (organic) and matter, by establishing the primacy of the laws which anticipate everything.

2. *Intelligence and Indiviadual Differences*

"The criterion of an intelligent response is being able to take the shortest route," Wheeler begins. He is, of course, referring to his law of least action, the law of parsimony, and that intelligence is related to the organism's ability to respond to the natural guiding momentum the law provides in solving problems, from rats in mazes, to mathematicians solving complex equations.

"Intelligence is to be equated with insight," he says in agreement with the questioners' probe. "The same thing." It is to be remembered that Wheeler also equates insight with learning. Insight, to him, is the seeing something whole. Would he then mean that intelligence is seeing many things whole or perhaps everything whole?

"Intelligence grows. I don't believe in native endowment." He was to say later in a separate conversation that you cannot sample any such thing as latent intelligence any more than one could sample the essential water by dipping a cup in a flowing river. He is convinced that organisms are not endowed with a fixed intelligence "in the germ plasm".

The three causal factors in intelligence are heredity, but far less than most American geneticists (at that time) were willing to admit, laws of growth and engineering, and the third, the environment. When he says environment he is not simply referring to socio-cultural influences, but also physical influences such as barometric pressure, temperature and other natural phenomena.

"The only way to measure intelligence is in achievement," he would say. "Anything on the order of potential is never measured. The only thing you can measure is action. It is kinetic energy and not potential energy. Potential energy, as he seemed to understand it, had no identity.

Individual differences, to Wheeler, are due to the laws of heredity, the laws of growth and the environment. "The laws work together to produce an organism. You can't have an organism unless you have all three."

Wheeler sees the genes as merely setting energies in motion. It is strikingly influential in his scheme, for they forge and direct the genetic energies in particular and individualized ways to produce uniqueness and specificity in organisms.

He also places great influence on environments, particularly the natural physical environment determined by climate, weather and geography.

3. *Learning*

"Learning is a succession of inventions which we call the growth of insight, the growth of understanding, the growth of intelligence and it is anything but mechanical. It is anything but conditioned. The only place in the picture where conditioning comes in is the stimulus has to be there to challenge the person to stir him up, put him in a state of imbalance"... so that he will apply his own energy along the line of development of some kind.

Wheeler has taken the trouble to eliminate dualisms from his system, always by means of incorporating the dualisms into a prior system of natural or organismic laws. He speaks of a low level intelligence operative prior to stimulus events in a particular environment. It is almost a metaphoric God having turned on the power switch and the universe is humming, prepared to provide energy on call.

An organism is confronted with a stimulus. The organism draws on the energy supply within its system to accomplish a solution to the problem engendered by the stimulus. It might be supposed that intelligence is a factor of the efficient means with which the organism makes use of the organismic laws to solve the problem, to mature, to learn, to gain insight, to grow – any of the word descriptions Wheeler uses to refer to the same phenomenon.

It's a "... matter of development, a matter of growth. It's a matter of maturation. It is an unfolding. It is a development. It is a series of discoveries, a series of emergencies, a series of developing of new capacities, new achievements." He is like a writer of fiction, a greeting card verse writer, a field naturalist in his description of learning, but he can be more specific.

"... then, he (the learner) comes to the ... problem." In this case its a rat in a maze. As he passes through the maze, not seeing the problem whole, the rat solves the problem of each small box through reliance on organismic laws and natural energies. "That's why his performance is trial and error because he can't see the whole thing. It is beyond his comprehension and he does solve, without any trial and error, separate little problems he confronts in succession by the simplest means that he can."

Wheeler's concept of *pace* is critical in learning, for an interactive exchange of maturity, or growth, together with active experience are key to learning.

While Wheeler does not say this, the writers might venture that the organism is in self-conscious consideration of experience. The product of such interaction is small insights and the solution of small problems which has been driven by the necessity of seeing the problem whole. See Appendix C and D.

4. *Memory and Forgetting*

Wheeler is consistent and specific in his view of remembering and forgetting. To remember is to return to time/place in as literal a way as possible. Because of the primacy of the whole, total recall is impossible. People are missing, sensory data are missing, unique phenomena of remembered moments may not find replication in the present. The organism is left with an imperfect recreation of experience. "... if and when you have confronted with enough similarity in the stimulus pattern to generate it", memory occurs.

There is no trace necessary at all. It is just re-creation of experience, not completely, because you do not repeat the situation completely. "We may partially re-create experience by means of language. Now we have one means of re-creating original situations without going back to them physically. There is language. Here is the nearest that I come the behaviorist. We have a large part of our previous environment still existing symbolically in our language so we think of those words like vacation or mountains or Mount Shasta that takes us back there."

It would seem that forgetting is related to diminished stimuli necessary to the re-creation of the experience.

5. *Evaluation*

One can only presume that Wheeler would test learning in behavior. The rat solves the problem of a path through the maze. The golfer scores par on a hole, a child performs on the piano. But that is never quite clear with Wheeler in the conversation nor in the writing. Insight is to be equated with learning, he says over and again.

"Oh, I see it now!" one might explain. Like Henry Higgins says of Eliza Doolittle, "By George, I think she's got it!" Eliza speaks a sentence after the fashion of a posh lady. She has perhaps "learned" to imitate the language pattern and inflection of another person. She has not replaced her own learned one. She has accomplished the behavior once. Has she learned? The connectionist would send her off to practice and reinforce her muscle memory. The behaviorist would continue reinforcement of the new behavior and through withdrawal of reinforcement extinguish the old behavior. Wheeler is satisfied as is. The organism will be able to sustain the change as long as it maintains the relationship between growth and action inherent in the pacing process.

To Wheeler one might "have it", with understanding but might not "behave it" constantly. For him one will have learned, however.

Wheeler surely makes a genuine distinction between mindless memorisation, wherein one might reproduce a given word, sentence or stanza, and true insight. In fact, the blind, practised ability of Eliza Doolittle would hardly qualify as insight for him. Then what would constitute acquisition of insight and how would it be truly recognised? What would be the difference between pseudo-insight and fully achieved insight? How could it be determined in some cases without regress to conscious/unconscious apologetics? Evaluation for Wheeler might well be a complex undertaking indeed.

IV. Relationship of Theories

Skinner makes his opinion of gestalt, or more precisely, the particular form of gestalt called field theory, perfectly evident in the interview. "I don't see anything in field theory." He concedes that perhaps he has not been taught to "look closely", but "I have never felt they have done anything but name some problems and these problems are of interest to us, but then solutions are not because they tend not to be real solutions." He says that, "We can teach a child to observe, to attend to details, to organise materials" without field principals. He goes on to say that his idea of repertoires may be something like "continuous field" but do not appeal to "forces operating in these fields."

Presumably he suspects a form of vitalism in gestalt thinking, perhaps like Wheeler's notion of energy or "low intelligence." Actually Skinner does not seem to have a need for any extraneous psychological thinking in his radical behaviorism. Perhaps the great weakness in Skinner is that his system explains everything. There is no falsification possible.

But so does Wheeler's. Wheeler, when he does refer to other systems, tends to regard them as "the others". He makes little distinction between behaviorism and connectionism but rails against psychologies riddled with the problem of dealing with dualisms, and the necessity for mechanistic explanation of phenomena.

And yet a comparison of their views generates many interesting similarities. Not surprisingly, both regard human beings as representing a point on a biological continuum. Each agrees that organisms tend to respond regularly. Wheeler, however, develops his Laws of Human Nature which hold primacy in the behavior of organisms.

Neither is sympathetic to any concept of "fixed mind". Both feel that intelligence is a dynamic concept manifest in behavior, and, growth is possible. Both are optimistic, in terms of the human organism's potential to change, learn, and grow.

There would seem to be critical difference between Skinner and Wheeler when comparison of learning theory is considered. It begins in attitude of world view. Skinner is concerned with authority and control. He has the sense that personkind has always been controlled, has always been shaped by contingencies with no freedom, by which he means choice or will, and no dignity, in that, with no choice, people become products of the stimulus/response environments in which they grew. He therefore urges populations conditioned to moderation, through cooperative planning, as preferable to control inflicted by malevolent external forces. Radical behaviorism offers the learning theory necessary for that control. It suggests deliberate choice of contingency environments and selection of reinforcable behaviors. Undesirable behaviors would become extinguished by deliberate elimination of reinforcement. In its pure form, it might be Skinner's *heavenly city* but hellish to many others, especially those who, to Skinner, represent highly individual, selfish personalities, for whom life in a cooperative society would be a prison.

There is none of this control emphasis in Wheeler. From 1938 until the end of his life he was interested in his world cycle explanation for global behavior of populations, but he was not interested with respect to controlling a world condition. Rather, he was interested in understanding it, and perhaps, through such understanding, adjusting to it, deriving such benefit as possible and reducing the harm by anticipating threat. Wheeler was that consummate gestaltist, a total world ecologist, seeing the interrelatedness of everything, not only in the world, but in the universe. At the end, Wheeler was overwhelmed, by his almost mystical, though not superstitious, fascination with a dynamic, organismic view of reality.

If one believes in emergence, in growth, in maturation, in unfolding, in discoveries, new capacities as explanations of learning, it would seem doubtful that he would be greatly concerned with control.

There are, in spite of differences, similarities in their learning theory. It seems to the writers that Skinner's series of operants, as the intermediate units between defined behaviors, are very close to Wheeler's "small discoveries". Skinner's whole is new behavior envisioned and defined. Wheeler's whole is in the mass action or energy which derives out of his organismic laws. To Wheeler, the future is in the present, and the future is in the past, in the sense that, forces set in motion (an apple dropping) have an inevitable conclusion. Change can occur to modify the conclusion and might, with strategic awareness of the totality, and with selective intervention. (Someone catching the apple in flight, a hurricane wind disturbing the path, a huge suction slowing and stabilising the apple's descent, Magic.)

It is not to say that Skinner has no sense of large wholes, and more complex phenomena that he might observe or measure. In fact, one could conceive a total universe of interactive stimulus/response phenomena, operating to shape individuals and matter. In later papers Skinner suggests a Darwinistic theory of survival of the behavioral fittest, selection by behavior, with himself as the twentieth century Darwin. He is not so blind as to deny that there may be micro-behavior, subtly effective stimulus/response outcomes (as in so-called body language). He is concerned with keeping things simple, content with observation or regularised behavioral outcomes that satisfy rather traditional empirical strategies. Build, from what you don't know, to what you know satisfies the experimental Skinner. Beyond that, who is to say? No one who ever met him (or read his autobiography, for that matter) would deny a romantic hero version of the great man.

V. Inference for Classroom Teachers

Classrooms have always been extremely inefficient places. They have often been places where no one had any real idea of what changes were
desired in the students, little consciousness of the values and hence behaviors
to be engendered.

Education is involved with two major concepts: values cum behavior,
that is, value driven behavior, and change. Without a clear vision of what
behaviors are desired and little modern knowledge of change methodology, teachers are at some disadvantage. They muddle through without
much confident control using essentially vestigial remnants of seventeenth
and eighteenth century faculty psychology or imperfectly derived leftovers
of Lockeian and Herbartian apperceptive psychology.

What would a Skinnerian classroom look like? The teacher would be
armed with a specific knowledge of behaviors to be reinforced and behaviors
to be extinguished. All activity in the school would resemble *Walden Two*
so that contingency environments would maximise the naturally reinforcing options and the human interaction would be generative of selected
reinforced and extinguished behaviors. The classroom would be a techno-
logically modern environment of computers and multi-media wonder-
ment. All data would be available on call by the teacher or individuals on
internet. There would be no omissions and no mistakes. All the epistemological stuff would be painlessly and parsimoniously transferred. Depend-
ing on the level of sophistication of the media, teachers might stimulate
dialectical activity between students and students, students and teacher,
students and machines, teacher and machines, machines and machines.
Maybe there would be no teachers at all; too inefficient, too insufficient.

The writers are serious here. But does Skinner have usefulness to
teachers inefficient and insufficient as they might be? Skinner says if you
want positive change, recognise and reinforce small changes in behavior
that move toward desired behavior. Negative reinforcement, aversive in all
its complex forms, from physical beatings to emotional beating can *prevent*
behaviors, but will not develop positive behavioral change. Skinner says
arrange the contingencies so that students will be operating in naturally

reinforcing environments. Skinner says make the operant units small enough so that students always "get it right". Skinner assumes no natural preclusions to learning in any child. All children can and will learn if the circumstances are right. Skinner arranged (or selected) contingencies of reinforcement that generated his own personal fulfilment. Learning and growth were mostly desired and painless for him because he controlled the order and pacing of his growth, or so he claimed. Teachers can arrange these things for students. Too often schools and procedures are the opposite of Skinner's methods. They are painful, unpleasant, unreinforcing, menacing, selecting places where ill defined elites emerge and ill defined rejects fail. Skinner would wish for better.

In consideration of what Wheeler and gestalt thinking generally might provide for classroom teachers one must remember that it has already had its major impact. One might as well inquire what ever happened to progressive education as to what ever happened to gestalt. Hilgard has suggested that there are three possibilities: 1. It has been disproved and rejected; 2. It has been absorbed; 3. It has been neglected.

Cremin (1961) felt that progressive education (and hence, many gestalt principles) have been absorbed into standard educational practice. Hilgard agrees and cites many examples: Discovery method is a gestalt idea. Project method, much of child development theory, holistic reading instruction, study skill (SQ3R) techniques, the concepts of motivation, insight, of unfinished phenomena stem from gestalt. American style core curriculum, that is, planned interdisciplinary studies is gestalt inspired. Hilgard also suggests that because Wheeler moved away from his interest in organismic psychology, and that neither he, nor any followers, continued with confirming experimental work, Wheeler's ideas fell into neglect. Hilgard was particularly impressed with the Wheeler concept of pacing. There is much in Wheeler to be of use to modern teachers.

Wheeler would say, provide stimulation to excite the necessity to action on the part of students toward the solution of problems. Wheeler would say, encourage and allow time for maturity to interface with action, as in his concept of pacing. One is always behind the other and growth can result only as the two, maturity and action fuse. Wheeler would therefore say that patience is necessary in students and teachers. Insight cannot simply be called out. The stimulus conditions can create an environment for insight to occur, but cannot guarantee it on demand.

Wheeler would say drill and practice without insight, without maturity is wasted time. Wheeler would say that the experience of insight is so generative, so satisfying, it creates empowering access to natural energy toward seeking additional insights.

Wheeler would say that learning is easy and natural if it is attuned to the natural law of particulars and individuation arising out of mass action. Learning is, in such cases, the unfolding of inevitable growth. Wheeler would say, "Read my books. Allow the ideas contained therein to mature and relate to your personal action and experience. Skinner would probably say, as they all used to say in Susquehanna, Pennsylvania, "Hogwash!"

Notes on Source Material

SKINNER

As previously noted, it is the intent of the writers to provide some assistance in locating sources which will further develop and explain the content of the Skinner and Wheeler interviews. Texts and periodicals which relate directly to the questions and issues raised in the interviews are identified here with a brief commentary on the content of the texts.

Complete bibliographies of Skinner's work – texts, articles, audio tape – are readily available. For example, Daniel Bjork's recent biography, *B.F. Skinner* (1993) contains such a listing. *Skinner for the Classroom* (1982) edited by Robert Epstein contains a bibliography of books and papers published by Skinner through 1981. Skinner's own texts usually contain a bibliography of his work through the publication date of the text under examination.

Skinner's high rate of productivity has resulted in the publication of a large volume of material potentially useful in furthering an understanding of the content the interview. The publications cited in the annotations include fifteen published works. The three volume autobiography, *Particulars of My Life* (1976), *The Shaping of a Behaviorist* (1979), and *A Matter of Consequence* (1984), have been included in the study as they provide personal references which illuminate Skinner's theory and proposals. They do not, however, deal with the content of the interviews as directly as some of the other publications. Individual journal articles and published presentations have not been included as four of the volumes included in the annotations are collections of papers and presentations largely published previously to their inclusion in these texts – *Cumulative Record* (1959), *Reflections on Behaviorism and Society* (1978), *Upon further Reflection* (1987), and recent issues in the *Analysis of Behavior* (1989. The items included in these four volumes provide a substantial sampling of Skinner's papers. The texts which were selected as most relevant to the Skinner interview are listed here in order of publication.

Skinner, B.F., *The Behavior of Organisms: An Experimental Analysis*. New York: Appleton-Century-Crofts, Inc. 1938.

— *Walden Two*. New York: The Macmillan Company, 1948.

— *Science and Human Behavior*. New York: The Macmillan Company, 1953.

— *Verbal Behavior*. New York: Appleton-Century-Crofts, Inc., 1957.

— with Charles Ferster, *Schedules of Reinforcement*. New Jersey: Prentice Hall, Inc. 1957.

— *Cumulative Record*. New York: Appleton-Century-Crofts, Inc., 1959.

— and J.G. Holland, *The Analysis of Behavior: A Program for Self-Instruction*. New York: McGraw-Hill, 1961.

— *The Technology of Teaching*. New York: Appleton-Century-Crofts, Inc. 1968.

— *Contingencies of Reinforcement: A Theoretical Analysis*. New York: Appleton-Century-Crofts, Inc. 1969.

— *Beyond Freedom and Dignity*. New York: Alfred A. Knopf, 1971.

— *About Behaviorism*. New York: Knopf, 1974.

— *Reflections on Behaviorism and Society*. New Jersey: Prentice Hall, 1978.

Epstein, Robert (editor), *Notebooks of B.F. Skinner*. New Jersey: Englewood Cliffs, Prentice Hall, 1980.

Skinner, B.F., *Upon further Reflection*. New Jersey: Prentice Hall, Inc., 1987

— *Recent Issues in the Analysis of Behavior*. Columbus, Ohio: Merrill, 1989.

About Behaviorism is a good starting place for the non-professional psychologist to gain a basic understanding of Skinner's principles of the study of human behavior. Indeed, it may well serve the fledgeling psychologist, whose understanding of behaviorism is based on a knowledge of J.B. Watson and Pavlov. For, as Skinner points out in the preface to this work, Watson lacked factual support for many of his assertions and both Watson's and Pavlov's treatment of reflex was compatible with "the nineteenth century conception of a machine." This view he notes was "not corrected by the stimulus – response psychology which emerged during the next three or four decades." *The Technology of Teaching* (1968) addresses directly the problems and concerns of those responsible for instruction, and along with *About Behaviorism*, provide both suggested theory and practice related to instruction.

Although *About Behaviorism* was written well after the interview contained here, the text provides the basic data and frame of reference which will extend the information in the interview. In the introduction to *About Behaviorism*, Skinner (1974) p. 3 notes that: "Behaviorism is not the science of human behavior; it is the philosophy of science."

The beginning student of behaviorism should not be put off by this statement, thinking that a volume with a scientific or practical focus would be more helpful in gaining an understanding of Skinner's position.

Particularly helpful is Skinner's identification of common misconceptions about behaviorism. The text itself addresses these misconceptions and the final chapter, "Summing Up", responds to each of the misconceptions directly. This book does not provide a detailed discussion of the technology of teaching, a topic that commands considerable attention in this interview. It does, however, provide data which supports the teaching machine concept as well as data relating to teaching and the field of education generally.

The Behavior of Organisms: An Experimental Analysis (1938) is focused on the scientific study of behavior and is representative of the standard psychology text often encountered by novices in psychology and related fields of human development.

As the reader views Skinner's writing chronologically, the autobiographical works excepted, Skinner's increasing emphasis on the need for humans to change their environment as a step toward the solution of global problems is clear. Therefore, one finds Skinner relating psychological principle and social concern.

The appearance of *Walden Two* (1948), a novel, delineates clearly Skinner's extension of his experimental study to all realms of human life and reveals in detail the implications of Skinner's proposed solution to the personal problems as well as the society in general. *Science and Human Behavior* (1957) reflects both interests, the experimental study of human behaviour as well as the design of culture.

Verbal Behavior (1957) and *Schedules of Reinforcement* (1957), written with Charles B. Ferster, are technical in their approach. *Verbal Behavior* presents an analysis of verbal behavior including some traditional approaches to the problem as well as from Skinner's point of view of scientific analysis. Generally its chief concern is that of "prediction and control of verbal behavior". *Schedules of Reinforcement* (1957) describes a series of experiments which examine the relationships between subject's behaviour and the determination of subsequent behaviour as well as the prediction of reinforcement schedules.

Cumulative Record (1959) is a collection of papers originally published and/or presented elsewhere. The papers cover a wide range of topics appropriate for both the specialist and the general reader interested in human behavior. Part I, "The Implications of a Science of Behavior for Human Affairs, Especially the Concept of Freedom", Part II, "A Method for the Experimental analysis of Behavior – It's Theory and Practice, It's History and a Glimpse of It's Future," and Part III, "The Technology of Education" are of particular relevance to the content of this interview.

The Analysis of Behavior: A Program for Self-Instruction (1961) written with James G. Holland is a self-instructional textbook designed for use in an introductory psychology course. The material in the text was originally developed for use in a teaching machine. This programmed text provides an example of a type of instructional material which was developed in a number of fields and levels during the 1960s and early 1970s.

The Technology of Teaching (1968) focuses on the teaching process and the way in which machines may be employed to enhance the teaching-learning experience. The principles discussed in the interview are applied to the instructional setting.

Beyond Freedom and Dignity (1971) deals with the problems of human-kind as it copes with the dilemmas of the modern world as well as those foreshadowed. Skinner examines the phenomena of freedom, dignity, punishment and values as they effect human behaviour and offers the reader an exposition of his theory as it relates to the management of contingencies in personal lives, government and society. Chapter 7, "The Evolution of a Culture", and Chapter 8, "The Design of a Culture", are particularly pertinent to the interview.

Reflections on Behaviorism and Society (1978) is a collection of papers and presentations published between 1972 and 1978. The collection is divided into four parts: I. Science, II. The Science of Behavior, III. Education, and IV. A Miscellany. Section III, Education, is particularly pertinent to this interview; however, Chapters 1. "Human Behavior and Democracy;" 2. "Are We Free to Have a Future;" 3. "The Ethics of Helping People;" 4. "Humanism and Behaviorism;" and Chapter 8, "Why I am Not a Cognitive Psychologist" contain some material related to the interview and are also of concern to those interested in some of the recent developments in learning theory and curriculum theory.

Notebooks, edited by Robert Epstein, is a collection of selected notes ranging over a diversity of topics of both personal and professional interest to Skinner. A few of these notes relate to the content of the interview. The major portion of the notes consist of jottings of ideas, anecdotes, and observations which reveal a behaviourist's view of the scope of human behaviours. *Notebooks* serves as an interesting supplement to Skinner's main body of work. Although of interest itself, it does not provide the expository material a reader unfamiliar with Skinner's work would require to understand the core of his work.

Between 1976 and 1983, B.F. Skinner wrote a three-volume autobiography, *Particulars of My Life* (1976), *The Shaping of a Behaviorist* (1979), and *A Matter of Consequences* (1983). They are of interest to anyone who is seeking information about Skinner and the factors which influenced the course of his life both professional and private. The last volume, *A Matter of Consequences* (1983), contains commentary on the public and the scholarly communities' reception of *Walden Two*, the development of teaching machines, and the publication of his many books and articles as well as participation in public forums.

Upon Further Reflection (1987) is similar to *Reflections on Behaviorism and Society* in that both are collections of papers and presentations covering a variety of subjects. The papers included in *Upon Further Reflection* were published and/or presented between 1981 and 1986. Skinner indicates that there is no central theme in the book "beyond the commitment to an experimental analysis of behavior and its use in the interpretation of human affairs." (preface, p. vii)

The papers are organized into five sections: Global Issues, The Origins of Behavior, Current Issues in Psychology and Education, Behavioral Self Management, and For Behavior Analysts Only. Chapter 8, "The Shame of American Education" in section III, is of particular interest to educators as it examines teaching and the impact of current psychology on teachers and classroom behaviour. Emphasis is given to the influence of cognitive psychology on practice and proposed solutions to educational problems. A reading of the entire collection permits exploration of the link between Skinner's thinking and the daily life of twentieth century western societies. Because education is a key social institution many references to education, both problems and practice, are contained in all of the papers.

Recent issues in the Analysis of Behavior (1989) appears to be intended for readers who already have some knowledge of the field. Divided into three sections, Theoretical Issues, Professional Issues, and Personal Issues, the text is a compilation of papers previously published between 1987 and 1989 except chapters 8 and 23. The text is of particular interest in that a number of the chapters provide a more recent view of issues raised in earlier works. The student of Skinner's work should have no difficulty in acquiring any of the texts mentioned here. In addition, contemporary scholars have produced biographies, criticisms, and studies of Skinner's work which are many in number and readily attainable.

WHEELER

The publications cited in the annotations of the Wheeler interview include his five books published between 1929 and 1940. Among the many papers and monographs published by Wheeler, seven articles published between 1923 and 1935 in the *Psychological Review* and the *Journal of Educational Research* have been included in this study as they deal directly with the content of the interview and provide interesting points of contrast with many of Skinner's assumptions. In addition, they reveal the broad base of Wheeler's thinking as well as make specific applications to instructional and educational issues. Wheeler's publication activities did not cease in 1940. His work did, however, take a different turn exploring the relationships of world climate and human behavior as well as that of climate and and the prediction and understanding of business cycles. After his death, a group of Wheeler's friends and former colleagues published one of his notebooks, *Climate: The Key to Understanding Business Cycles*, edited by Michael Zahorchak (1983).

Books:

Wheeler, Raymond Holder, *The Science of Psychology*. New York: Thomas Y. Crowell Company, 1929, 2nd edition, 1940.
— *Readings in Psychology*. New York: Thomas Y. Crowell Company, 1930.
— *The Laws of Human Nature*. Cambridge: At the University Press, 1931.
— and Theodore Perkins, *Principles of Mental Development*. New York: Thomas Y. Crowell Company, 1932.

Periodicals:

Wheeler, R.H., "Introspection and Behavior", *Psychological Review*, Volume XXX, 1931.
—, F. Theodore Perkins and S. Howard Bartley, "Errors in Recent Critiques of Gestalt Psychology I. Sources of Confusion", *Psychological Review*, Volume XXXVIII, 1931.
—, — and — "Errors in the Critiques of Gestalt Psychology II. Confused Interpretations of the Historic Approach", *Psychological Review*, Volume 40, No. 3, 1931.
—, — and — "Errors in the Critiques of Gestalt Psychology III. Inconsistencies in the Thorndike System", *Psychological Review*, Volume 40, No. 4, 1931.
Wheeler, Raymond Holder, "Organismic vs. Mechanistic Logic", *Psychological Review*, Volume XLII, 1935.

— "A Set of Postulates for Educational Theory I. The Background", *Journal of Educational Research*, Volume XXVII, No. 5, January 1935.
— "Postulate for a Theory of Education II. A Methodology for Educational Research", *Journal of Educational Research*, Volume 29, No. 3, November 1935.
— "Climate and Human Behavior", *Encyclopedia of Psychology*, Philip Lawrence Harriman (editor),. New York: Philosophical Library, 1946.

R.H. Wheeler's first book, *The Science of Psychology, An Introductory Study* (1929), provides a survey of the study of human behavior from an organismic point of view. In the preface, Wheeler indicates:

> In the author's judgment the newer psychological texts have for the most part erred on the side of too great simplicity and brevity. Students often complete a semester or even a year of psychology without a real introduction to the subject and with almost no conception of psychology as a science.
>
> Wheeler (1929, p. vii

Therefore, Wheeler treats the general topics normally included in introductory psychology texts – Social Behavior, Intelligent Behavior, Emotive Behavior, Learning Behavior, Simple Reaction and Observational Behavior and the Nervous System in its Relation to Behavior – within a historical perspective as well as calling upon the then current research.

The summary set out the assumptions relating to the study of human behavior which were developed throughout the text describing the organismic view as it shaped the thinking of the author.

> The view of behavior held throughout the text led to important consequences. It is called the organismic view because any performance of the intact, total organism is emphasized as an organic whole. Accordingly, behavior at large consists of events or activities best defined by the most obvious and dominating of the conditions which control it, the conditions are social. The organismic view suggested the fundamental law in terms of which to interpret behavior, the law of least action; it also made a physical as opposed to a psychic conception of behavior unnecessary because action and energy were regarded as neutral terms implying neither matter nor mind.
>
> Wheeler (1929) p. 506

Many of the themes introduced in this text are developed further in subsequent works. *Readings in Psychology* (1930) was published as a companion volume to *The Science of Psychology* (1929). Its purpose is that of "giving the beginning student in psychology access to a selected number of experimental investigations," Wheeler (1930) preface. The organization of the readings corresponds to the organization of *The Science of Psychology*, including two readings by Wheeler, and one by Wheeler and his colleague at the University of Kansas, Thomas D. Cutsforth. The editor's notes prefacing each of the readings provide content for the interview notes and commentary.

If one were to read only one text by Wheeler, *The Laws of Human Nature* (1931), would be most productive in promoting an understanding of the organismic position and Wheeler's unique contributions to the growth of the study of human psychology. Chapters II–III, "The Background of Contemporary Psychology", "The Transition to Scientific Psychology", and "Biological Organization" reveal the Wheeler sense of excitement and adventure given his participation in what he views as a revolutionary movement:

> The revolution in science, however, is so broad in its implications that it cannot be regarded as progress in science alone. Rather, it illustrates an evolution in human thought that is certain to affect profoundly the culture and destiny of the civilized world.
>
> Wheeler (1931), p. xi

Wheeler sees the construction of radical theories – relativity movement in physics, the organismic movement in biology, and the gestalt movement in psychology – as contributing to the development of a new "method of thought" which will break down "the conventional barriers between psychology and the other sciences." Wheeler (1931) p. xii.

Wheeler traces the development of basic ideas in Western thought from Greek dualism to the twentieth century building a context for the emergence of the organismic point of view. He identified gestalt psychology as the way out of the "dead end" created by atomism in modern psychology as typified by connectinism and behaviorism. Thus, relying on the physicists' laws of dynamics, as do most gestaltists, Wheeler identifies and explores the ramifications of the "laws of human nature" for the study of the science of human behavior.

Principles of Mental Development: A Textbook in Educational Psychology (1932) by R.H. Wheeler and Francis T. Perkins achieved prominence in its day and remains one of the classics in the field. The text provided the psychological undergirding the progressive movement in education serving as a major text in teacher education programs. Wheeler and Perkins define their task as that of incorporating developments in Gestalt psychology, organismic studies in biology and relativity in physics in such a way that the thinking generated by these newly developing areas would prove useful for prospective teachers.

A sense of mission pervades the text as the authors seek to achieve the presentation of:

> ... a Psychology for Education which relates the facts of experiment to the demand of the growing mind to live not only efficiently, but with artistic and moral expression. ... Psychology has yet to realize that it is the Science of Human Nature, not the science of sensations, reflexes, mechanical conditioning processes and bundles of urges. It has yet, in general, to make the discovery that man is NOT a machine, that the laws of his behavior are the laws of intelligence, will and personality, not the laws of association.
>
> Wheeler and Perkins (1932), p. ix

The text, then, is synoptic in nature treating a broad range of topics in the field of educational psychology – the laws of human nature, the nervous system in relation to behavior, the learning process, mental development, perception and thinking, intelligence, emotion and will, personality, motivation, memory, discipline, procedures in education.

> The student of Educational Psychology must realize that, whether he wills it or not, he will be an engineer of human nature. He should be prepared to face the larger problem of his task as the laws of human nature demonstrate them to be ... . In the interest of these larger and more important problems for Education, conventional material on sensory processes and the physical conditions of mental work have been omitted. It is more important that the prospective teacher knows about motivation than the laws of color mixture, and the shape of Pacinian corpuscles.
>
> Wheeler and Perkins (1932), p. xi

Wheeler and Perkins acknowledge their debt to Kurt Koffka and Robert M. Ogden. Their text demonstrates the application of Koffka's and Ogden's work to educational theory and practice.

The second edition of Wheeler's 1929 text, *The Science of Psychology: An Introductory Study*, was published in 1940. A re-ordered and extended version of the original text, the second edition includes significant additions of reports of experimental data supporting Wheeler's position.

Wheeler points out that the work of the great intellectual geniuses of the Western World – Grotius, Copernicus, Galileo, Kepler, Descartes, Harvey, Spinoza, Boyle, Newton, Locke, Leibnitz and others – laid the cornerstone for the phenomenal progress of civilization. This progress has forged ahead of "understanding" and has produced problems in all phases of human life. He identifies psychology as the science which provides an avenue to an understanding of the social order as:

> ... psychology is the science of human nature, it examines human motives, the springs of action. It seeks to know how motives determine behavior, to learn which of these motives are basic and which are secondary; how motives can be increased when they are insufficient, how they can be decreased when they are too powerful – all in the interests of peace and harmony in the social order and balance within the personality of the individual.
>
> Wheeler (1940), p. 3

Neither Wheeler, nor Skinner for that matter, considered the traditional psychology as an adequate science. Skinner speaks of a science of human behavior. Wheeler, caught up in the enthusiasm of the gestaltist, also considers the old psychology replaced with a science based on the logical principles of his organismic method.

The organization of *Science of Psychology*, then, reinforces his commitment to study individual human behavior within the broader context of the social order. Thus, the author is true to organismic psychological principles both in the structure of the text as well as its content.

Wheeler's five books are out of print. Fortunately, they are still accessible through university libraries in the United States as are the monographs and periodicals included in the bibliography. The writers did not locate any biographical material other than that inlcuded in the various biographical dictionaries and personal information obtained through university personnel files, archives and colleagues.

Notes on Hilgard's Estimate
of Wheeler's Organismic Position

It was noted in the preface that the 1948 edition of Ernest R. Hilgard's *Theories of Learning* provided an organizer for the thinking of the writers as well as criteria for the selection of the psychologists to be interviewed. Hilgard had, in the 1948 edition, devoted an entire chapter to the work of R.H. Wheeler. The text which has subsequently been published in four editions, the fourth and fifth with Gordon H. Bower, is a basic reference for students of learning theory. It became a point of considerable curiosity to the interviewers when it was discovered that the chapter on Wheeler's organismic psychology, a major chapter in the 1948 edition, had been omitted in subsequent editions.

In Hilgard (1956) the following note was included in chapter 7, "Classical Gestalt Theory":

> Their views (Koffka, Lewin and Wertheimer) were picked up considerably modified by Wheeler (1929) (1932) (1940) under the name of organismic psychology, but his position deviated too much from the classical gestalt psychology for him to be counted in the core group.

In a note appended to the statement above, Hilgard continues

> ... Wheeler's views were elaborated with Perkins, in widely used textbook on educational psychology, Wheeler and Perkins (1932). For an account of the organismic position, see the first edition of this book Hilgard (1948), pages 234–260. Because Wheeler's theory is no longer influential, the chapter has been dropped from this edition, despite some provocative ideas contained in the theory.
> Hilgard (1956), p. 225

A brief reference to Wheeler's work appears in chapter 7, and another in chapter 10.

In Hilgard and Bower (1966), the authors include in the preface a note explaining the omission of the chapter entitled: "Lewin's Field Theory". The authors state that ...

> [Lewin's] views on learning have not been sufficiently influential in recent years to justify this attention to them in the context of learning theory.

The note which follows was appended to that statement.

> It may be recalled that the views of Raymond H. Wheeler which were represented in the first edition were omitted from the second. Lewin's views are currently very much alive in social psychology and in relation to some aspects of human motivation. Lewin's views as represented in the second edition have not been specifically challenged or refuted; the earlier chapter is still an acceptable introduction to them.

Hilgard and Bower (1966), p. 259, make a reference to Wheeler in relation to learning rates and pacing. Another reference is made to Wheeler and Perkins (1932), p. 322, in the chapter, "Functionalism", noting Wheeler and Perkins' alternative theory to consolidation theory. No mention of Wheeler was included in either the 1975 or 1981 edition of Bower and Hilgard.

Hilgard edited *Theories of Learning and Instruction*, the sixty-third yearbook of the National Society for the Study of Education (1964). The text includes a chapter by Hilgard, "The Place of Gestalt Psychology and Field Theories in Contemporary Learning Theory", in which he notes that when preparing the 1956 edition of *Theories of Learning* he indicated that "research on or related to the position (Wheeler's) was no longer sufficient to call for a new chapter." (p. 65) He comments further on Wheeler:

> Does this mean that the ideas which seemed so fresh when Wheeler and Perkins presented them in 1932 are valueless in 1964? Not at all; it means that something was wrong with the manner in which the ideas were developed, so that strong contemporary defenders are not to be found.
>
> Hilgard (1964), pp. 65–66

Further, Hilgard indicated in that chapter that he believed that Wheeler's position as a psychologist was diminished by his research and writing on the influence of wet and dry weather cycles on behaviour and what Hilgard viewed as Wheeler's "exaggerated claims". The work to which Hilgard refers was an extensive research program undertaken at the University of Kansas and continued for approximately thirty years at Kansas as well as Babson College in Massachusetts. While at Kansas, the project received assistance from the National Youth Authority which provided a total of 96 students who assisted Wheeler in the collection of data and the development of his "big book". Wheeler mentions this phase of his research in the interview. Wheeler left the University of Kansas for personal reasons. Whether or not events at this time had significance on his later career awaits further consideration.

Hilgard (1964) and Hartman (1935/1974) in more detail, provide chronologies and explanation of the fall of gestalt psychology from a position of prominence during the rise of progressivism in American education to that of a peripheral role at the present time.

In the interview included here, Wheeler is highly critical of his fellow psychologists for their failure to rely on logic and clear thinking when identifying questions to be studied and drawing conclusions from experimental data. His fellow psychologists, on the other hand, are equally critical of the gestalt psychologists in general for the failure to test their thinking through extensive experimentation and for their utilization of untested personal experience as justification for a theoretical position.

According to Hartman (1935/1974), psychologists representing alternative positions found gestalt psychologists personally difficult to deal with as well as flouters of conventional psychological practice, a serious barrier to communication in any professional field. The contrast in the careers of Skinner and Wheeler relative to their reception by their peers, their place in the history of psychology, the implications of their work for education and their respective places on the world stage is dramatic.

Wheeler's Laws of Human Nature

For a complete listing and description of these laws, see Wheeler (1931), pp. 70–92.

1. *The Law of Field Properties*
   Any item of reality is in its own right an integrated whole that is more than the sum of its parts.

2. *The Law of Derived Properties*
   Parts derive their properties from the whole.

3. *The Law of Determined Action*
   The whole conditions the activities of its parts.

4. *The Law of Individuation*
   That parts emerge from wholes through processes of differentiation or individuation.

5. *The Law of Field Genesis*
   Wholes evolve as wholes.

6. *The Law of Least Action*
   Objects generally move from one place to another over the shortest route in time, action being defined as energy multiplied by time.

7. *The Law of Maximum Work*
   When the balance of an energy system is disturbed, the energy of the entire system is affected and all the available potentials are expanded, that is, become kinetic, in the process of re-establishing the balance.

8. *The Law of Configuration*
   The idea that never does one discrete and isolated event affect another discrete and isolated event; for discrete and isolated things are fictions ... any reaction of the human being is a reaction of the organism-as-a-whole, and is a unified response to a total situation of some kind.

Diagram Comparing Skinner and Wheeler's Learning Theories

SKINNER

(Old) Behavior

Desired
(New) Behavior

Intelligence a factor of the speed of change in this process and the ability to sustain change

incremental selected change observed		incremental selected change observed		incremental selected change observed		incremental selected change observed	
A $\xrightarrow{}$	A^1	$\xrightarrow{}$	A^2	$\xrightarrow{}$	A^3	$\xrightarrow{}$	B
operant 1		operant 2		operant 3		operant 4	
	Immediate positive reinforcement		Immediate positive reinforcement		Immediate positive reinforcement		Immediate positive reinforcement
							RESULT Desired new behavior manifest and observable

A^1, A^2 and A^3 represent the movement towards desired new behavior observed and reinforced. In life these behaviors and changes happen in nature. In radical behaviorism they are selectively observed and positively reinforced.

See pp. 44–54 for narrative description.

WHEELER

(Old) Behavior	Preferable (New) Behavior

Movement driven by low energy "intelligence" along self determined parsimonious route (A^1, A^2, A^3)

$$A \longrightarrow A^1 \longrightarrow A^2 \longrightarrow A^3 \longrightarrow B$$

     small insight   small insight   small insight

Movement through small insights (A^1, A^2, A^3) grounded in natural law with parallel emergent maturity (pace)

RESULTING IN
Large insight
Discovery
Growth
Closure
Intelligence

Unlike in Skinner, the role of the change agent is less obvious. What does the agent really do expect to attempt to influence the nature of the experience?

See pp. 80–82, 91–95, for narrative description.

Bibliography

Barrie, J.M. *The Admirable Crichton*. London: Hodder and Stoughton, 1928.

Bjork, Daniel W. *B.F. Skinner*. New York: Basic Books, 1993.

Blakemore, Colin. *The Mind Machine*. London: Penguin Books, BBC, 1988.

Bode, Boyd. *Conflicting Psychologies of Learning*. New York, 1929.

Borring, E.G. and Lindsey G. *A History of Pyschology in Autobiography* (vol. 5), New York: Appleton-Century-Crofts, 1967.

Bossing, Nelson L. *Progressive Methods of Teaching in Secondary Schools*. Boston: Houghton Mifflin Company, 1942.

Bower, Gordon H. and Hilgard, E. *Theories of Learning*. Longwood Heights, New Jersey: Prentice Hall, 1981.

Bruner, Jerome. *The Process of Education*. Cambridge: Harvard University Press, 1960.

Burkhardt, Richard W.J. *The Spirit of a System. Lamarck and Evolutionary Biology*. Cambridge: Harvard University Press, 1977.

Catanis, Charles and Stevan Hainad, eds. *The Selection of Behavior, the Operant Behaviorism of B.F. Skinner. Comments and Consequences*. Cambridge: Cambridge University Press, 1989.

Cannon, H. Graham R.R.S. *The Evolution of Living Things*. Manchester University Press, 1958.

— *Lamarck and Modern Genetics*. Manchester University Press, 1959.

Child, C.M. "The Beginning of Unity and Order in Living Things"; *The Unconscious, A Symposiom*. (A.A. Knopf, 1928). Freeport, New York: Books for Libraries Press, Inc., 1966. Reprint Series.

Child, Charles Manning. *Patterns and Problems of Development*. Chicago: The University of Chicago Press, 1941.

Coghill, G.E. *Anatomy and the Problem of Behavior*. Cambridge: At the University Press, 1929.

Cremin, Lawrence A. *The Transformation of the School*. New York: Alfred A. Knopf, Inc., 1961.

Dewey, John. *Democracy and Education*. New York: The Free Press, 1916.

— *Interest and Effort in Education*. Boston: Houghton Mifflin Company, 1913.

— "The Reflex Arc Concept in Psychology", *Psychological Review*, vol. 3 (1896).

Edelman, Gerald M. and Vernon B. Mountcastle, *The Mindful Brain.* Cambridge, Mass. and London, England: M.I.T. Press, 1978.

Epstein, Robert (editor). *Skinner for the Classroom.* Champaign, Illinois: Research Press, 1982.

Farber, Susan L. *Identical Twins Reared Apart: A Reanalysis.* New York: Basic Books Inc., Publishers 1981.

Ferster, C.B. and B.F. Skinner. *Schedules of Reinforcement.* New Jersey: Prentice-Hall, Inc., 1957.

Feynman, Richard. *The Principle of Least Action in Quantum Mechanics.* Ph.D. Thesis, Princeton, 1942.

Fuller, R. Buckminster. *Critical Path.* New York: St. Martin's Press, 1981.

Gleick, James. *Chaos Making a New Science.* London: Heinemann, 1988.
— *Genius, The Life and Science of Richard Feynman.* New York: Pantheon Books, 1992.

Gould, Stephen Jay. *Bully for Brontosaurus Reflections in Natural History.* New York: W.W. Norton and Company, 1991.
— *The Mismeasure of Man.* New York: W.W. Norton and Co., 1981.

Guthrie, E.R. *The Psychology of Human Conflict.* New York: Harper, 1938.
— The Psychology of Learning. New York: Harper, 1935.

Hartmann, George W. *Gestalt Psychology. A survey of facts and principles.* Reprint of 1935 ed. published by Ronald Press Co. Westport, Connecticut: Greenwood Press, 1974.

Hernstein, Richard J. and Charles Murray, *The Bell Curve.* N.Y.: The Tress Press, 1994.

Hilgard, Ernest R. *Psychology in America A Historical Survey.* New York: Harcourt Bruce Jovanovick, Publishers, 1987.
— *Theories of Learning.* New York: Appleton-Century-Crofts, 1948.
— *Theories of Learning.* New York: Appleton-Century-Crofts, second edition, 1956.
— *Theories of Learning and Instruction.* The Sixty-third Yearbook of the National Society for the Study of Education. Chicago, Illinois: The University of Chicago Press, 1964.
— and Gordon H. Bower. *Theories of Learning,* third edition. New York: Appleton-Century-Crofts, 1966.

Houghton, Raymond W. "The Focus of Humanism and the Teacher", *Humanizing Education, The Person in Process.* Addresses at the 22nd A.S.C.D. Annual Conference Dallas, Texas, 1967, Robert Leeper (ed.) Washington, D.C.: Association for Supervision and Curriculum Development, N.E.A., 1967.

Huxley, Aldous L. (1932) *The Brave New World.* New York: Harper and Row, 1969.

Itzkoff, Seymour, *The Decline of Intelligence in America.* Westport, Conn.: Praeger, 1994.

Jackson, David S. "Babes in Byteland", *Time*, August 22, 1994, Vol. 144, No. 8.

James, William, *Talks to Teachers on Psychology and to Students on Some of Life's Ideals*. New York: Henry Holt and Co., 1899.

James, William, *Principles of Psychology*. New York: Holt, 2 vols, 1890.

Jaynes, Julian. *The Origin of Consciousness in the Breakdown of the Bicameral Mind*. Boston: Houghton Mifflin Company, 1976.

Jennings, H.S. *The Biological Basis of Human Nature*. New York: W.W. Norton & Company, Inc., Publishers, 1930.

— *Suggestions of Modern Science Concerning Education*. New York: MacMillan, 1920.

Joravsky, David. *The Lysenko Affair*. Cambridge, Mass.: Harvard University Press, 1970.

Jourdain, Philip E.B. *The Principle of Least Action*. Chicago: The Open Court Publishing Company, 1913.

Koestler, Arthur. *The Case of the Midwife Toad*. London: Hutchinson and Company, 1971.

Koffka, Kurt. *Growth of The Mind*: An Introduction to Child Psychology, London: Routledge and Kegan Paul, 1921.

Kohlberg, Lawrence, *The Philosophy of Moral Development: Moral Stages and The Idea of Justice*. San Francisco: Harper Row, 1981, Vol. 1.

Köhler W. *The Mentality of Apes*. New York: Harcourt Brace, 1917.

Krutch, Joseph W. *The Measure of Man: On Freedom, Human Value, Survival and the Modern Temper*. New York: Grossett and Dunlap, 1954.

Lamarck, Jean-Baptiste, *Philosophie Zoologique*. Paris: Dentu, 1889.

Lane, David and Brian Stratford. *Current Approaches to Down's Syndrome*. London: Holt, Rinehart and Winston, 1985.

Leadbetter, David. *The Golf Swing*. London: Harper Collins Publishers, Ltd., 1990.

Loeb, Jacques. *Comparative Physiology or The Brain and Comparative Psychology*. (trans. Anne Leonard Loeb). London: Progressive Science Series, 1901.

Lyons, William (Editor). *Modern Philosophy of Mind*. London: Everyman, 1995.

McLuhan, Marshall. *Understanding Media*. New York: McGraw-Hill, 1964.

Mead, George Herbert. *Mind, Self and Society*. Chicago: The University of Chicago Press, 1937.

Medvedev, Zhores A. *The Rise and Fall of T.D. Lysenko*. (Trans. G.L. Michael Lunn with editorial assistance of Lucy G. Lawrence.) New York: Columbia University Press, 1969.

Ogden, Robert M. *Psychology and Education*. New York: Harcourt Brace, 1926.

Osborne, R. Travis. *Twins: Black and White*. Athens, Ga.: Foundation for Human Understanding, 1980.

Packard, Alpheus S. *Lamarck*. New York: Longmans Green, and Co., 1901. Reprinted by Arno Press, Inc., 1980.

Pavlov, Ivan P. *Conditioned Reflexes.* (trans. G.V. Anrep). Oxford: Oxford University Press, 1927.

Price, Charles. "As Though it had eyes", *Golf Digest.* May 1993.

Rushton, J. Philippe. *Race, Evolution and Behavior.* New Brunswick, New Jersey: Transaction Publishers, 1994.

Russell, Bertrand. *An Outline of Philosophy.* London: Allen and Unwin, 1927.

Skinner, B.F. *About Behaviorism.* New York: Alfred A. Knopf, 1974.

— and J.G. Holland. *The Analysis of Behavior: A Program for Self-Instruction.* New York: McGraw-Hill, 1961.

— *The Behavior of Organisms.* New York: Appleton-Century-Crofts, Inc., 1938.

— *Beyond Freedom and Dignity.* New York: Alfred A. Knopf, 1971.

— *Contingencies of Reinforcement; A Theoretical Analysis.* New Jersey: Prentice Hall, Inc., 1969.

— *Cumulative Record.* New York: Appleton-Century-Crofts, Inc., 1959.

— with Margaret E. Vaughan. *Enjoy Old Age.* New York: Knopf, 1983.

— *A Matter of Consequences.* New York: Alfred A. Knopf, 1983.

— *Notebooks.* Robert Epstein (editor), Englewood Cliffs, New Jersey: Prentice Hall, 1980.

— *Particulars of My Life.* New York: Alfred A. Knopf, 1976.

— *Recent Issues in the Analysis of Behavior.* Columbus, Ohio: Merrill Publishing Co., 1989.

— *Reflections on Behaviorism and Society.* Englewood Cliffs, New Jersey: Prentice-Hall, Inc., 1978.

— with Charles Ferster. *Schedules of Reinforcement.* New Jersey: Prentice Hall, Inc., 1957.

— *Science and Human Behavior.* New York: The Macmillan Company, 1953.

— *The Shaping of a Behaviorist.* New York: Alfred A. Knopf, 1979.

— and Robert Epstein (editor). *Skinner for the Classroom.* Champaign, Illinois: Research Press, 1982.

— *The Technology of Teaching.* New York: Appleton-Century-Crofts, 1968.

— *Upon Further Reflection.* New Jersey: Prentice-Hall, Inc., 1987.

— *Verbal Behavior.* New York: Appleton-Century-Crosts, Inc., 1957.

— *Walden Two.* London: Collier-Macmillan Limited, 1948.

Soyer, Valery H. *Lysenko and the Tragedy of Soviet Science.* (trans. by Leo Gruliow and Rebecca Gruiliow). Brunswick, New York: Rutgers University Press, 1994.

Spencer, Herbert. *The Principles of Biology*, Vol. 1. New York: D. Appleton and Company, 1896.

Terman, L.M. "The Influence of Nature and Nurture Upon Intelligence Scores." *Journal of Educational Psychology*, 1928, Vol. 19.

— *The Measurement of Intelligence.* Boston: Houghton Mifflin, 1916.

Thompson, Travis. "Benedictus Behavior Analysis: B.F. Skinner's Magnum Opus at Fifty", *Contemporary Psychology*, 1988, Vol.33, No.5.

Thorndike, Edward L. *Human Learning*. The Messenger Lectures Cornell University Fifty Series 1928–29. New York: The Century Co., 1931.

Twain, Mark. *Letters From the Earth*. Bernard Devoto (ed.). New York: Harper & Row Publishers, 1962.

Watson, J.B. *Behaviorism*. New York: Norton, 1924.

— *Psychology From the Standpoint of a Behaviorist*. Philadelphia: J.B. Lippincott, 1919.

Watson, Peter. *Twins An Uncanny Relationship?* New York: The Viking Press, 1982.

Wertheimer, M., *Productive Thinking*. New York: Harper 1945.

Wheeler, R.H. "Climate and Human Behavior", *Encyclopedia of Psychology*. (Philip Lawrence Harriman, editor). New York: Philosophical Library, 1946.

— *Climate: The Key to Understanding Business Cycles*. (With a Forecast of Trends into the 21st Century), Michael Zakorachax (editor). Jupiter, Florida: Tide Press, 1983.

—, F. Theodore Perkins, and S. Howard Bartley. "Errors in Recent Criticisms of Gestalt Psychology I. Sources of Confusion", *Psychological Review*. Vol. 38, 1931.

— and F. Theodore Perkins. "Errors in the Critiques of Gestalt Psychology III: Inconsistencies in Thorndike's System", *Psychological Review*, Vol. 40, No. 4, July 1933.

—, F. Theodore Perkins, and S. Howard Bartley. "Errors in the Critiques of Gestalt Psychology IV: Inconsistencies in Woodworth, Spearman and McDougall", *Psychological Review*, Vol. 40, 1933.

— "Introspection and Behavior", *Psychological Review*, Vol. XXXV, 1923.

— *The Laws of Human Nature*. Cambridge: At the University Press, 1931.

— "Organismic vs. Mechanistic Logic", *Psychological Review*, Vol. XLII, 1935.

— "Persistent Problems in Systematic Psychology v. Attention and Association", *Psychological Review*, Vol. 35, No. 1, January 1928.

— "Postulates for a Theory of Education II. A Methodology for Educational Research", *Journal of Educational Research*, Vol. XXIX, No. 3, November 1935.

— and Theodore Perkins. *Principles of Mental Development*. New York: Thomas Y. Crowell Company, 1932.

— "The Problem of World Climate", *Bulletin American Meteorological Society*, Vol. 21, 1940.

— *Readings in Psychology*. New York: Thomas Y. Crowell Company, 1930.

— *The Science of Psychology*. New York: Thomas Y. Crowell Company, 1929.

— *The Science of Psychology*, 2nd edition. New York: Thomas Y. Crowell Company, 1940.

— "A Set of Postulates for Educational Theory I. The Background", *Journal of Educational Research*, Vol XXVIII, No. 5, January 1935.
Wilson, Edward O. *On Human Nature*. Cambridge, Mass. London: Harvard University Press, 1978.
Zusne, Leonard. *Biographical Dictionary of Psychology*. Westport, Conn.: Greenwood Press, 1984.
Zusne, Leonard. *Names in the History of Psychology*. Washington, D.C.: Hemisphere Publishing Corporation, 1975.

UNPUBLISHED MATERIALS

Letters – Clark University Library
To: Dr James P. Porter, Dean Clark College from H.M. Kelley, New York Manager, The Fisk Teachers' Agencies, April 12, 1915.
To: Prof. E.S. Conklin, University of Oregon, Eugene, Oregon from J.P. Porter, April 15, 1915.
To: Dr J.P. Porter from Raymond H. Wheeler, August 20, 1916, University of Oregon.
To: Dr R.H. Wheeler from: unsigned, Spetember 7, 1916 ... could be Porter.
To: Dr J.P. Porter from Raymond H. Wheeler, University of Oregon, October 25, 1916.
To: Dr J.P. Porter from Raymond H. Wheeler, University of Oregon, January 27, 1917.
To: Dr Raymond H. Wheeler, University of Oregon from J.P. Porter, Clark University, February 21, 1917.
To: Dr J.P. Porter from Raymond H. Wheeler, Camp Bowie, Fort Worth, Texas, May 5, 1912.
Clark College Monthly, 1912.

College Records
Transcript of academic work in the Department of Psychology, Clark University, September 1912 to June 1915.
Report of the examination of R.H. Wheeler, June 10, 1915, thesis title: *An Experimental Investigation of the Process of Choosing Passes*
Biographical summary by Helen Tatum written in 1927, University of Kansas.
Unsigned statement re: Wheeler's work at the University of Kansas.
Biographical Sketch from the University of Kansas files by Wheeler, *c*.1932.

Index